THE POWER OF HONOR

The Power of Honor is the best Christian book I have read this year. In fact, it is one of the best Christian books I have *ever* read. A terrific writer and thinker, Fawn Parish illumines an aspect of God's character that we rarely think about. Honor is not optional in a healthy Church or society — but we're not healthy. Consumed with our own egos and agendas, we have forgotten how to honor God and our fellow man. This book helps to reverse this destructive trend by teaching us what honor is, why it is essential and how we can extend it to others.

GEORGE OTIS, JR.
Founder and President, The Sentinel Group
Lynnwood, Washington

A spiritual treasure and great power are waiting to be discovered in this unusual message. You will be delightfully surprised — and blessed.

BILL BRIGHT
Founder, Campus Crusade for Christ
Orlando, Florida

This book can change the way you think and live. Fawn Parish issues a clarion call to restore the honor and dignity God wants us to show to all people, thus releasing a healing dynamic with great spiritual potency.

DUTCH SHEETS
Author of *Intercessory Prayer*
Pastor, Springs Harvest Fellowship
Colorado Springs, Colorado

Prayers are rising up from the Body of Christ worldwide in an unprecedented way. Fawn Parish helps us to see those for whom we pray with "eyes of honor." This book will help you pray with even greater power as you heap the matchless grace of Christ on others.

DAVID BRYANT
Founder and President, Proclaim Hope!
New Providence, New Jersey

I am delighted to honor Fawn Parish for sharing how humility — one of our greatest needs — is worked out in honoring what God honors. Written with stark honesty and a compelling, engaging style, this book is destined to help bring to fulfillment our Lord Jesus' prayer that His body of believers will become one.

JOY DAWSON
Author of *Intimate Friendship with God* and *Intercession*
Tujunga, California

Fawn Parish has written a message that the whole Body of Christ needs to read. It is insightful, challenging, and touches the heart. *The Power of Honor* is destined to be a classic that will be read from generation to generation.

CINDY JACOBS
Author of *Women of Destiny*
Cofounder, Generals of Intercession
Colorado Springs, Colorado

Honor is a tattoo, not an accessory; it must be etched on the soul of the practitioner. Fawn Parish's insights about this truth drew me to examine its design in the plan of God. Without honor, writes the author, restored relationship between men and women is not possible. When Deborah and Barak sang a due — not a solo — they founded a greater destiny.

JANE HANSEN
Author of *Fashioned for Intimacy*
President, Aglow International
Edmonds, Washington

This book is as easy to read as it is joyous to practice. Don't be surprised if your life becomes fun again as expressions of honor begin to lift your everyday relationships to the level of a celebration. Don't be surprised if God renews your ambitions for the healing of the nations with a vision of people as being not merely needy, but in God's sight wonderfully worthy of our honor.

STEVE HAWTHORNE
WayMakers
Austin, Texas

For a culture grooved by the impact of cynicism, nihilism and self-centeredness, *The Power of Honor* is a prophetic wake-up call that I believe will serve as a redemptive healing balm to the wounded spirit of the church and society.

REV. MARK POLLARD, SR.
President, Common Ground Coalition
Atlanta, Georgia

THE
POWER
OF
HONOR
learning to love well

Fawn Parish

[CONVERSATIONS]

a division of Reignbridge, Camarillo, California, U.S.A.

Published by Conversations
A Division of Reignbridge
Camarillo, California, U.S.A.
Printed in U.S.A.

Reignbridge seeks to embrace, engage, and educate,
emerging leaders in impacting culture by extending the
fame and renown of Jesus. Join the conversation!
www.powerofhonor.com

All Scripture quotations, unless otherwise indicated, are taken from the *New American Standard Bible*, © 1960, 1962, 1963, 1968, 1971, 1972, 1973, 1975, 1977 by The Lockman Foundation. Used by permission.

KJV — *King James Version*. Authorized King James Version.

NIV — Scripture quotations are taken from the *Holy Bible, New International Version®*. Copyright © 1973, 1978, 1984 by International Bible Society. Used by permission of Zondervan Publishing House. All rights reserved.

NKJV — Scripture taken from the *New King James Version*. Copyright © 1979, 1980, 1982 by Thomas Nelson, Inc. Publishers. Used by permission. All rights reserved.

NRSV — From the *New Revised Standard Version* of the Bible, copyright 1989, Division of Christian Education of the National Council of the Churches of Christ in the United States of America. Used by permission.

RSV — From the *Revised Standard Version* of the Bible, copyright 1946, 1952, and 1971 by the Division of Christian Education of National Council of the Churches of Christ in the USA. Used by permission.

TLB — Verses marked (*TLB*) are taken from *The Living Bible* © 1971. Used by permission of Tyndale House Publishers, Inc., Wheaton, IL 60189. All rights reserved.

Cover Design by www.timmyroland.com
Interior Design by Rob Williams
Edited by Deena Davis

Library of Congress Cataloging-in-Publication Data
Parish, Fawn. 1956-
The power of honor / Fawn Parish.
    p.   cm.
Includes bibliographical references.
ISBN 0-8307-2381-1
1. Honor — Religious aspects — Christianity.   2. Christian life.
I.   Title.
BV4647.H6P37   1999
241' .4 — dc21   99-25908
                                                                          CIP

Dedication

This book is dedicated to Joey, Joel, Lynn and Celia.
If I ever doubted the honor God has given me,
all I'd have to do is look at you.

Contents

Foreword by John Dawson		11
Acknowledgments		13
Introduction: Two Words That Could Change the World		15
Chapter One	The High Cost of Dishonor	19
Chapter Two	The Source of All Honor	35
Chapter Three	Honor Given to Man	45
Chapter Four	Honoring God's Word	57
Chapter Five	Honor in Prayer	71
Chapter Six	Honoring the Bride	83
Chapter Seven	Honoring Diverse Cultures	95
Chapter Eight	Honoring Cities	109
Chapter Nine	Honor Between Men and Women	123
Chapter Ten	Honoring Difficult People	137
Chapter Eleven	Honoring Children	151
Chapter Twelve	Honoring Old Age	167
Chapter Thirteen	Honoring the Helpless	179
Chapter Fourteen	Honor in Language	191
Chapter Fifteen	The Color of Worship	205
Appendix A	Praying by Listening	215
Appendix B	Covenant of Unity	217
Appendix C	Our Hands Are Stained	221

Foreword

I admit to an obsession. I want the Church to act like Jesus. I long for people to see God's perfect love and turn to Him. Who will lead us? Who has the intensity needed to deliver us from the spiritual death that emanates from passionless religious habits? Who really knows God?

I recommend *Honor* for three reasons. First, its impact on me; second, because I admire the author; and third, because the core content captures what God is saying to the redeemed in Christ, worldwide.

I serve a movement called the International Reconciliation Coalition, a growing network of Christian reconcilers working in the troubled places of the earth. The wounds of the nations are incurable without grace from God—grace that could be released by anyone following the teachings in this book. Based on the Bible and Fawn's profound experiences, these are principles that, if followed, could release a flood of healing into your relationships and ultimately into your city.

Fawn Parish is a modern Deborah. Known for wise counsel, she is one of the most respected Christian leaders in the northwest cities of the Los Angeles area. Honored by religious, political and cultural leaders alike in her homeland, Fawn also influences the direction of the world prayer movements through involvement in Concerts of Prayer and the Reconciliation Coalition.

Fawn has given us a great gift. I found myself consuming each paragraph like a man eating delicious food. Have you ever read words that gave form to the deep things seen by your spirit? As your mind comprehends, your heart leaps in agreement. This is the mark of writing done under the influence of the Holy Spirit.

This is a very original work, yet Fawn has gathered a treasure trove of quotes from the great saints of history to complement her wonderful Bible teaching. Humorous and easy to read, yet filled with wisdom, she answers the question, What does love look like? Worth reading for the pithy anecdotes and dramatic stories alone, Fawn paints pictures with words that are hope filled, refreshing and heart transforming.

Seeing our culture through the eyes of Jesus, Fawn teaches us how to restore relationships through the giving of honor. This simple activity goes to the heart of the mystery revealed in the cross of Jesus. Humility and brokenness expressed as gratitude produce restoration in others.

Jesus commanded us to make disciples. What are you doing with your circle of influence? Reading this book could mean the difference between fruitfulness or barrenness. I for one need to be reminded that Jesus' example of leadership runs totally contrary to our culture. His life shows me that success is not measured by how many people I control but by the number of people I have released into their full potential, the number of people I once led who now surpass me. This book shows me how. I need to read this teaching once a year or perhaps enjoy a chapter a day for devotional meditation. I can guarantee you one thing: You will be a better leader, parent, manager, married partner or friend because you took this journey into truth.

John Dawson
Founder
International Reconciliation Coalition

Acknowledgments

C. S. Lewis once asked, "Is any pleasure on earth as good as a circle of Christian friends by a good fire?"[1] I have warmed my soul often by the sacred fire of many a valued friend. Some of them I've never met: A. W. Tozer, Eugene Peterson, Walter Wangerin Jr., C. S. Lewis, Annie Dillard, Hudson Taylor, Brother Lawrence. Their words have inflamed my soul and ignited my passion to know Jesus more intimately.

Others I have known in person: Lynn McMahan, Stuart and Celia McAlpine, John Dawson, David Bryant, Steven Hawthorne—all passionate lovers of Jesus, who have greatly influenced my thinking. They, too, burn with intensity and sacred fire.

But the world could not exist if made up solely of prophetic thinkers and dreamers. There is the hallowedness of everyday life. Friends who have made this book possible by practical spirituality include Carey Nosler, Shari Burnett, Mike and Lynn McMahan, Lionel Kimura, Jamey Brooks and my beloved husband, Joey. They invested a lot of muscle and sweat equity into seeing this book to birth. They hammered away and spent long hours into the night, building a place called Gracebridge, while I wore two hats. I was supposed to be the general contractor. Their work freed me to steal away often and write. Without them, this book would not be.

My darling son, Joel, put up with a preoccupied mom more often than I'd care to admit. Joel extended grace to me beyond his years. His spontaneous hugs and kisses always produced at least another paragraph when I was feeling dry and uninspired.

My mom deserves thanks for raising me without television. She pushed me headlong into books. And there were hundreds of spiritual classics lying about, begging to be read. It was because of her that I learned to savor the deliciousness of words.

I am rich with beloveds who have given me their time, wisdom and unswerving friendship. God has indeed honored me to sit by His fire with His friends and listen to His stories.

Note
1. C. S. Lewis, *Letters of C. S. Lewis,* (New York: Harvest Books, 1988).

Two Words That Could Change the World

A few years back I was ready to speak for a National Day of Prayer event when I heard God's typical out-of-the-blue-not-on-the-subject whisper. He said, "I want to restore the word 'honor' to My people." While trying to figure out what this meant, and what I was supposed to do about it, I remembered a picture God had given me months before while praying with some friends. I had seen a doctor with a stethoscope dangling around his neck, stooped over and wagging his finger in the face of a man at his feet. The man was looking up for help. The doctor held behind his back a vial full of red liquid. His voice dripped with disdain as he said to the man, "You are sick...sick...sick."

I knew immediately that the doctor represented the Church. The red vial stood for the blood of Jesus—the cure for all ills. The man at the doctor's feet was the world, looking in vain for help while the Church smugly diagnosed death.

I understood this to be a chilling picture of the self-righteous posture the Church has sometimes taken toward the world. At times we have unleashed Satan's arsenal of dishonor, heaping blistering attacks on our perceived cultural enemies.

Instead of modeling the prodigal father, who was just itching to wrap a rich robe around his stinking son and throw him a party, the Church has stood with its arms folded across its chest. Often we have moved only to point fingers.

Our smugness is as current as last night's news. Not long ago I watched in anguish the funeral of a young gay man who was beaten to death in Laramie, Wyoming. In the midst of grieving relatives and friends, Christians (their pastor was interviewed on television) were holding placards that read, "AIDS is the cure for fags." As they shouted obscene slogans, they seemed clueless as to the source of their hatred.

It wasn't always this way. In the Roman Empire, the Early Church used to hide under bridges and catch discarded babies flung over the side. They would take the babies home to love and nurture them. This happened so repeatedly that the Romans said of the Early Church, "They love our own more than we do."[1]

Today I believe that God is restoring this kind of love to His people. He is turning "pointing fingers" into outstretched hands that heal. Voices that once dripped with disdain are beginning to bless. Hearts that once were brittle and calloused are becoming pliable and tender. God is changing us by giving us the gift of an enlarged heart. We are beginning to wash non-Christians' feet instead of airing their dirty laundry. We are finding our former stance of accusation odious and are choosing to become people who bless their cities and neighborhoods with practical, tangible servanthood. We are no longer content to be simply diagnosticians; we are becoming people who cure.

One of the ways God is enlarging the Church is by restoring the word "honor" to our vocabulary. Pastors are making covenants to honor and not speak ill of one another. Men are beginning to acknowledge and honor the spiritual gifts of women. Diverse cultures are finding pleasure in honoring each other and worshiping together. We are beginning to value the significance of each other. Strong men are weeping in repentance for trivializing and marginalizing those who are different from them. We are beginning to see that just as Jesus is the glory and the glorifier, He *is* honor; and that honor flows from Him to every man, woman and child on the face of the earth.

Just in case we miss the point, God's Word tells us that He has honored us, and continues to honor us in every moment of our existence. We were honored at birth by being made in His image; we are honored by His cleansing blood that gives us a relationship with Him; we are invited to receive and to give unceasing honor in heaven, world without end. If you love and obey God, you are fast approaching a future that is dense with honor. It's what eternity is all about.

TWO LIFE-CHANGING WORDS

Not only is honor what eternity is all about, it is how God designed all of our relationships to function here on earth. C. S. Lewis, in his book *The Weight of Glory*, says, "You have never talked to a mere mortal." He explains that statement this way:

> The dullest and most uninteresting person you can talk to may one day be a creature...you would be strongly tempted to worship, or else a horror and corruption such as you now meet only in a nightmare. All day long we are helping each other to one or the other of these destinations. It is in light of these overwhelming possibilities...that we should conduct all our dealing with one another, all friendships, all loves, all play, all politics....Nations, cultures, arts, civilizations—these are

mortal, and their life is to ours as that of a gnat. It is immortals whom we joke with, marry, snub and exploit—immortal horrors, or everlasting splendors.[2]

If honor was the basis of how we thought and acted toward one another, imagine the possibilities! If we began to regard each other with the significance that God Himself regards us, imagine how life would change! Such musings are not simply extravagant impossibilities, they are the very ambition and intent of God. In fact, He commands us to "honor all" (1 Pet. 2:17).

This is a book about those two words: "Honor all." It is not an exhaustive study on the subject, it is simply an introduction, a primer as it were. However, our exploration would be inadequate if we did not discuss the high price of dishonor and its consequences. So, we will begin there. It is a sad place to start, because often we are ignorant of our own history, while our victims are not. Because our dishonor has been so destructive, we will only look at it briefly. Then we will explore the wonderful source of all honor—God.

Throughout the rest of the book, we will discuss how to live out honor—how to be people of honor in thought, word and deed. It's a journey well worth taking. I am honored you're taking it with me.

Notes
1. Statement by historian Steven Mansfield, in his tape series "Church History in America." For an excellent overview of the relationship between technology and coming moves of God, you can order his series from Belmont Church, 68 Music Square East, Nashville, Tennessee, 37203 (615) 256-2123.
2. C. S. Lewis, *The Weight of Glory and Other Addresses* (New York: Macmillan, 1980), pp. 18, 19.

CHAPTER ONE

The High Cost of Dishonor

*Of all that was done in the past, you eat the fruit either
rotten or ripe....For every ill deed in the past
we suffer the consequence.*
—T. S. Eliot[1]

The priest thoughtfully poured soil back and forth between his
cupped hands, sifting a rhythm to his silent prayers. If soil could
speak, this soil would weep. This was the tenth massacre site the
prayer team had visited in the past two days—ten places where
God Himself had cried. It was here the Yamassee Indians ceased
to be a people, their life extinguished through ethnic cleansing
by settlers desiring more land. While no race has a franchise on
sin, and history is complex, it was clear to those present that
something unspeakable had happened here.

The small band of intercessors, who were visiting this site
to repent of the obliteration of the Yamassee nation, were
midway through an eight-hundred-mile prayer journey that
retraced Union Army General William Tecumseh Sherman's
trail of pillage, burning and rape through Georgia and the
Carolinas.[2]

Fern Noble, a prayer-reconciliation leader, paced back and forth, weeping, with her Bible open in her hands. For Fern, the desecration of this site was not just a historical fact. The blood of her own Native American people had saturated this soil. In deep anguish of spirit, Fern asked God a question she had been asking for many years: "Why do so few of my people believe You?"

The numbers are pitifully few. Less than 5 percent are Christians. Most, in fact 90 percent, have suffered from alcoholism. Suicide is five times higher for Native Americans than for any other ethnic group, and the average life expectancy is only 40.1 years.[3]

As she prayed and walked, Fern noticed a peculiar sight. A stack of papers seemed to grow on top of her open Bible. She asked the question again, "Why do so few of my people believe You?" The papers grew until they were a thick pile, obscuring the Bible laying flat in her hands.

"What does this mean, God?" she asked once again, waiting with childlike expectancy. Understanding came quickly. The growing stack of papers represented the treaties of the white man, which in essence had said to the Indian, "This is our covenant to you; this is our promise. You can trust what we say, for we have signed it. This is the word of the Great White Father in Washington. He cannot lie. You can trust that he will keep his word to you."

Some historians say that as many as eight hundred times we broke treaty after treaty with the Indians. In many cases the treaties were broken with unspeakable brutality. History records that the Sand Creek massacre, ordered by Colonel John M. Chivington, an ordained Methodist minister, slaughtered and mutilated over three hundred Native Americans, most of them women and children and some of them futilely clutching a white flag.[4] Other stories tell of a chief holding a treaty to his chest as he was mowed down by government troops.

In the hostile actions against tribe after tribe, in the confiscation of land, in the repeated lies of treaty upon treaty, the Great White Father's words were not honored.

When those who loved God came to the Native American and showed them the Bible, saying, "This is the covenant of God; this is His promise. You can trust what He says because He signed it in blood. This is the Word of the Great Father in the sky. He cannot lie. You can trust Him. He will keep His word to you," it was too late.

God's answer to Fern's question was unmistakably clear. Few Native Americans believed God because they couldn't see the Bible for all the broken treaties laying on top of it. To them the Word of God was just one more treaty, one more covenant, one more word of the Great Father that was never intended to be kept. The Native American would not be fooled twice.

Can our actions so misrepresent God that future generations do not trust or even consider Him and His claims? Can we destroy future receptivity to the gospel by our dishonor of people today? I believe the answer is a well-documented and agonizing yes. History is shot through with examples. In 1878, Janitin, a Kamia Indian from San Diego, gave this eyewitness account:

> I and two of my relatives went down...to the beach...to catch clams.... We saw two men on horseback coming rapidly toward us.... My relatives fled.... I was too late.... They overtook me and lassoed and dragged me for a long distance.... They locked me in a room for a week; the Father told me that he would make me a Christian.... One day they threw water on my head and gave me salt to eat, and with this the interpreter told me I was a Christian.... Every day they lashed me because I did not finish my work.... I found a way to escape...but I was

tracked, and they caught me like a fox.... They lashed me until I lost consciousness.[5]

Our dishonor toward the Native American is not simply a matter of the past. Even as recently as thirty years ago, Native American children were dragged from their families and placed in "residential schools." They were forbidden to speak their own language or observe their own customs.[6] In these schools, children were beaten and shamed for being Indian, many times in the name of Christ.

At the age of five, Lynda Prince, a Carrier-Sekani of Canada, was taken to a residential school where she was not allowed to speak her native language. "Assimilation taught us to become ashamed of who we are," she says. "Basically, it said, God made a mistake when He created you." Some children were carted off in a garbage truck, crying as they were torn from weeping parents, and taken to schools hundreds of miles away. My Canadian Cree friend, Carol, has told me of one former United Church residential school near Edmonton, where there are little crosses of children who died at the school. Carol believes that some of them died of a broken heart.

LEARNING FROM EACH OTHER

I was talking to Native American John Sanford, the author of *The Elijah Task*.[7] I said, "John, if we could rewind the tape of American history between the whites and the Native Americans, what could it have been? What would have pleased God?"

John said that among the Osage Indians, there was a tradition that was handed down, chief to chief. A chief, many years in the past, had a vision. In the vision he saw the white men coming in three stages. He saw white men with fire sticks, and they wer‹ trappers. The Indians were not to bother them. He saw white men come with picks and shovels (while there were no words for picks and shovels in the Indian language, he described their use). Even though these men would rape the earth, they were not to be bothered. Then the third group were the black coats. These, the Indian chief said, were people who knew the truth about God. They were to be listened to.

John's point was that the missionaries came to a people with eternity in their hearts. If only the missionaries had sat down in mutual humility and said to the Native Americans, "We know Jesus Christ; tell us what you know." Instead, they said, in effect, "You have nothing to offer us; we have everything to offer you." We "castrated" an entire culture with our unmitigated arrogance. That wound is still fresh today.

FAULT LINES OF HISTORICAL DISHONOR

Our legacy of dishonor has not been limited to Native Americans. The furrows of our error rake deeply through the heart of many generations and cultures. Most Christians, for instance, are unaware of the history of hate perpetrated on the Jews by the Church, yet almost every Jew can recall the facts in vivid detail.

Venomous hatred toward the Jews is strewn through the writings of respected Church fathers. In a vivid fantasy of the Last Judgment, Tertullian (c. 160–c. 230) gloats over the spectacle of the anticipated punishment of the Jews, at which time he will turn "an insatiable gaze" and taunt them with their rejection of Christ.[8] John Chrysostom (c. 347–407), one of the most honored of the early theologians, whose writings are considered by the Eastern Orthodox Church to be second only to Scripture, seemed to hate the Jews even more than Tertullian. In his *Oracions Against Jews*, Chrysostom calls them godless, idolaters, pedicides...stoning the prophets and committing 10,000 errors.[9] The Church's past is understandably a huge obstacle to Jews considering the claims of Jesus Christ. For many Jews, the Cross is akin to a swastika.

William Nichols, in his book *Christian Anti-Semitism*, reproduces a table by Raul Hilberg that compares the historical Church's canonical law, dating from A.D. 306 to 1434, with Nazi measures censoring the Jews, enacted from 1935 to 1942. The script appears to be written by the same diabolical hand.[10] Notice the dates of these three examples of canonical law from the Christian Roman Empire and the medieval Catholic world:

Jews and Christians not permitted to eat together, Synod of Elvira, A.D. 306.

The marking of Jewish clothes with a badge, 4th Lateran Council, A.D. 1215, Canon 68. (Copied from the legislation by Caliph Omar II [634–44], who had decreed that Christians wear blue belts and Jews, yellow belts.)

Compulsory ghettoes, Synod of Breslau, A.D. 1267.

Examples like these led one historian to write: "The road from here [canonical law] to Auschwitz may not be direct, but one can get there from here."[11]

The fault lines of dishonor spread through our history to other races as well. A friend of mine with a drywall business was repairing a wall when he noticed a picture with Japanese writing on it. He asked the lady who hired him about the picture. "You don't want to know," she replied. "Yes, I do," my friend softly said, realizing he was touching a painful memory. The woman poured out her story. In World War II she had been separated from her husband and interned in a Japanese relocation center, where she was raped. Though now in her eighties, the dishonor she had experienced over half a century ago still scratched its jagged nails across her soul.

What about the African-American community? I saw an interview with the son of the late Jackie Robinson, and my heart was moved as this soft-spoken man talked about his father. He said the fact that his dad had been hit by more pitches than the rest of the team combined was something he remembered more than his dad's batting average.

While our history as a Church has been at times glorious, and it is appropriate to honor Christians who have authentically loved others different from themselves, it is equally true that our history is full of dishonor and shame. The high cost of that shame is a terrible reality—entire cultures have been alienated from the welcoming grace and truth of Jesus Christ.

I have touched human ashes in the ovens of Auschwitz; I have listened in Jerusalem to a portion of the names read of over 1 million Jewish children killed in the Holocaust. As a Christian, my hands are not entirely free of blood. I can not selectively own history. Do I trust that two thousand years ago, on Golgotha, the Son of God intentionally died for humanity, and that event has present-day power? Absolutely. Do I believe that a long history of God's people dishonoring God when they dishonored others has ramifications today? I do.

DISHONOR
TOWARD GENDER

The dishonor of which I speak is not simply a matter of dishonoring race. We have equally excelled in our dishonor of gender.

Church father John Chrysostom called women "whitewashed tombstones," saying that inside they are full of filth, and that marriage was given to men to keep them from submitting to prostitutes.[12] Epiphanius (A.D. 315–403) claimed that the female was "easily seduced, weak and void of understanding. Masculine reasoning will destroy this female folly."[13] Tertullian blamed women for the death of the Son of God. "You are the devil's gateway; you are the unsealer of that forbidden tree; you are the first deserter of the divine law; you are she who persuaded him who the devil was not valiant enough to attack. You destroyed so easily God's image, man."[14]

Not long ago I was one of several facilitators of a gathering of prayer leaders in Southern California. The weekend was humming along when all of a sudden I suggested to the women leaders in the room that they join me in repenting of our attitudes toward male leadership. There was momentary silence.

When we all resumed breathing, God gently swept into the room. People cried and confessed their lack of trust and their feelings of being used and never taken seriously. One major leader wept as he washed the feet of a woman leader, confessing on behalf of men the attitudes of male superiority. He had identified with those pastors who viewed women in the Church as only potential volunteers for menial tasks.

God has a controversy with His people. We have significantly dishonored those whom God loves, and we may no longer sweep our dishonor under the rug. We cannot hide behind the skirts of ignorance. God is serious about exposing and correcting our error. The list of our grievous sins toward one another—culture to culture, gender to gender—could fill a well-stocked library. Yet, as I mentioned earlier, there is no race or gender with a franchise on sin. We have all sinned, and we have all been sinned against.

God is grooming a new generation of men and women who are committed, in humility, to a two-word command in Scripture: Honor all.

We could spend the rest of our lives trying to pin fault on one another, nursing our own woundedness and capitalizing on our victimization. We could live mired in bitterness and accusation. But God has not left us to ourselves. He is giving us strong courage to face the error of our ways. Like a skilled surgeon, He is revealing and removing our deep-seated malignancies. He is grooming a new generation of men and women who are committed, in humility, to a two-word command in Scripture: "Honor all." These two words could arguably encourage the openness of future generations to the splendor and power of Jesus Christ.

GOD'S COMMAND TO HONOR ALL

It is hard to imagine two simple words changing the way we live and think. But God can pack a universe into a sentence, a world into a word. God has given us two words in 1 Peter 2:17 that I believe are slated to become the modus operandi for the Church in the third millennium. In some versions of the Bible, the words are translated, "Honor all." The application of this bold command could significantly shatter hell's viselike grip on individuals and cultures and drastically affect how future generations view Christ and His claims.

Honor is a dynamic with spiritual potency. When honor is unleashed, it can reveal the heart of God to hardened individuals and to whole cultures, opening them up to their intended destiny of eternal intimacy with God.

Honor all. Like the command to pray without ceasing, it sounds hopelessly impossible to do. A whole swarm of questions hover like mosquitoes at a family picnic. Does God expect us to honor people who are not honorable? Can honor reveal the grace and truth of Jesus? What does honor have to do with Native Americans or Jews or Japanese or African-Americans, women, or any dishonored people? These are all good questions. Before we begin to answer them, we should define precisely what honor is and what it is not.

HONOR DEFINED

The word "honor" in the Greek means "to highly value, to prize, to not take lightly, to esteem, to give weight to, to ascribe worth." It is significant that the word "glory" in the Old and New Testament often shares the same definition as the word "honor."

The Bible gives us three levels of honor that are applied to man.[15] The first level is intrinsic honor. It is honor possessed by God and given to every human being. This honor is an attribute of God, and He freely bestows it on us simply by creating us in His image.

The second level is honor based on character.

The third level is honor based on performance.

Because there is so much unexplored terrain on the subject of honor, we will limit ourselves to the honor God gives to every person, regardless of merit, character or performance.

WHAT HONOR IS NOT

There are lots of inaccurate or incomplete ideas about honor. For instance, in America, we think of honor primarily in terms of merit. Honor classes are for the bright and academically motivated. We worship attractive film and television stars. We heap honor on skilled athletes, exalting them to godlike status. We honor successful businessmen and envy their savvy. We have borrowed frail (little g) gods from the Greco-Romans—gods of youth, beauty, and success—and we spend our money and time worshiping at their fickle altars. Inaccurate and incomplete notions of honor will never help us to obey God's command to honor all. Honor runs much deeper throughout the universe than receiving an Oscar or a Most Valuable Player title.

To understand honor, we must begin with this primary fact: The essence of honor is found in the personality and character of God. We can never understand honor apart from God because honor, like love, is defined in Him. He is honor personified. In fact, heaven can be described as one continual round of honor.

On the other hand, Satan personifies dishonor. He presides over a dominion of dishonor. He has much at stake in making sure our concept of honor remains radically skewed. For example, in Pakistan, "honor killings" take place daily; converts from Islam to Christianity are murdered by their families in order to retain the "honor" of the family.

Oriental societies live much of their lives ruled by the tyranny of "saving face," nervously measuring every action for the amount of honor or dishonor it will bring to the family.

In Mediterranean society, there is great concern with honor and shame rather than with individual guilt.[16]

In the Middle East, the honor of the extended family, its ancestors and its descendants is the highest social value. If the loss of honor (particularly of a female member) is widely known, other members of the family may feel "honor" bound to cleanse the family name. This cleansing can require the death of the offender.[17] Newspapers in Cairo and Saudi Arabia frequently carry stories of runaway sisters gone bad and the revenge that brothers or cousins pursue in the name of family honor.

Is it possible that "honor" has been so ill-defined because it is such a powerful, overarching spiritual dynamic? Has Satan so badly distorted the concept of honor because he is jealous of the honor God alone deserves and has bestowed on men? I think the answer is an unqualified yes.

WHAT HONOR IS

Honor is a holy feature of the heart and mind of God. It is something God uniquely possesses and personifies. In looking at Him, we recognize complete and utter worth. Honor is an attribute of God that commands recognition and is the most appropriate response to a genuine encounter with Him,[18] and it is a response that He alone deserves.

Those who know God, prize Him; they do not take Him lightly. Those who know Him best take great delight in speaking honor of Him.

There is no one else in the universe worthy of honor but God. He, whom hosts of heaven worship and demons grudgingly acknowledge as Lord, is without equal in glory. He is indescribably great. He is unexcelled in goodness. In the presence of God, all superlatives blush with inadequacy.

> "To whom then will you liken Me that I should be his equal?" says the Holy One. Lift up your eyes on high and see who has created these stars, the One who leads forth their host by number, He calls them all by name; because of the greatness of His might and the strength of His power not one of them is missing (Isa. 40:25,26).

All beauty, all goodness—everything that we have learned to understand as desirable—originates in the personality and character of God.

Is someone particularly kind? We only know kindness because God has been kind to us. Do we admire someone's generosity? We recognize it as generosity because we understand true generosity in the nature of God. Is someone's behavior especially marked by humility and servanthood? Jesus defined humility and servanthood by laying down His life for us. In honoring an admirable quality in someone, we are simply acknowledging a hint of the full and perfect attribute found in God.

God does not have gunny sacks of love, joy, peace, patience and gentleness heaped around the throne. He doesn't hear your prayer for truth and then take a big scoop and dip it into the truth sack and pour it down from heaven. He gives you Himself.

Truth is not an objective set of suppositions. It is a person. Love is not merely an emotion, it is a person. What are we honoring when we honor the wisdom of an individual? Jesus is the wisdom of God, and there is no wisdom apart from Him. Is someone honorable? It is important to realize that apart from Jesus, all notions of honor are nonsense. Make no mistake: *Apart from God, our virtue has no context.* Everything, including the way we think and act with each other, is meaningless.

My son, Joel, attends a public school where they emphasize a different character trait each month. Joel's teachers love kids, and we have been blessed to have them as a part of his education. Yet it hasn't seemed to dawn on anyone that character traits apart from God are pure mumbo jumbo. If there is no God—no good—who's to say that being discourteous is worse than being kind? If there are no moral absolutes, who's to say that Stalin or Mao or Hitler was wrong? If there is no God, no transcendent authority, where do we get the idea that some actions are right and some are wrong? Who's to say what behavior is desirable?

If nothing is absolute, then we are left with absolutely nothing. You might as well do as you please. If nothing is absolute, then hedonists are the only practical realists.

But if there is God, and He is the source of all excellence and honor, then all our ideas about what is good must originate from and be defined by Him. Scripture says, "Every good thing bestowed and every perfect gift is from above, coming down from the Father of lights, with whom there is no variation, or shifting shadow."[19] Everything we know to be good and perfect comes from God. He is the absolute source of all we know to be pure, clean, lovely, desirable.

HEAVEN'S MAIN PREOCCUPATION

Because of God's unsurpassed excellence, it is only natural that heaven's sole pleasure is to give honor to God. Honor is the native language of heaven. As Steve Hawthorne observes, heaven is one mighty preoccupation with honor.[20] In the book of Revelation, we see the Bride heaping honor on the Son, the Son on the Father, the Father back to the Son and the Son back to His bride. And then the whole process marvelously begins again and continues forever. It is one glorious circle that never ends.

Like mighty bagpipes, honor thrums unceasingly through eternity, sweeping up into a mighty crashing chorus, "You are worthy, O Lord, to receive glory and honor and power; for you created all things, and by Your will they exist and were created."[21]

The four and twenty elders can't help themselves. Every time they get a glimpse of God's majesty, His worth, His value, His weightiness and dignity, they find themselves once again face-down on the floor. Each glimpse is like a new revelation. Each time they see Him it's as if they've never seen Him before. The perfection of His beauty and glory can never be fully taken in.

The wonder is that this glorious, honorable God does an astounding, heart-stopping thing. He also crowns us—tragic, shattered earthenware that we are—with glory and honor. In a sweeping display of His generosity He gives us what He alone deserves. And He invites us to give this marvelous gift to each other.

Jesus,

> *You truly are the desire of the nations. You are the supremely honored One of all worlds. All heaven declares Your glory. All creation shouts Your worth. Every good and perfect thing finds its genesis in You. Nothing we desire compares with You. Riches, influence, pleasure—all of them heaped together do not equal the bliss of a moment with You. You are honor itself. And You have surprised us by sharing Your honor with us. We are speechless with awe. Amen.*

SCRIPTURES FOR MEDITATION
Psalm 8:5; Isaiah 40:25,26; James 1:17; 1 Peter 2:17; Revelation 4:10,11

QUESTIONS WORTH ASKING

- How does Peter's vision of the unclean animals in Acts 11:5 relate to this chapter?
- Is there any group of people or culture that you find difficult to honor?
- God has crowned man with glory and honor. Is this a universal statement or does it only apply to a few select people? How does it apply to you?
- In what way is the God of the Bible different from the gods of myth and legend?
- Is there a relationship between honor and pleasure?
- Every good and perfect gift comes from God. What are the good and perfect gifts God has given to you?

Notes

1. Quoted in Philip Yancey, *Praying with the KGB* (Portland, Ore.: Multnomah, 1992), p. 7.
2. Access the full report of the Operation Restoration prayer walk at http://www.geocities.com/heartland/Hills/6230/or.html.
3. John Dawson, *Healing America's Wounds* (Regal Books: Ventura, Calif.: 1994), p. 152.
4. Ibid., pp. 145-48.
5. Alvin M. Josephy Jr., *500 Nations* (New York: Alfred A. Knopf, 1994), p. 343.
6. In America, the forced removal of Native American children from their families was for the purpose of sending them to what were euphemistically called boarding schools. In Canada, the schools were called residential schools.
7. John Sanford, *The Elijah Task* (Wheaton, Ill.: Victor Books, 1977).
8. David P. Efronymson, "Tertullian's Anti-Judaism and Its Role in His Theology," Ph.D thesis, Temple University (Ann Arbor, Mich.: University Microfilms, 1977).
9. John Chrysostom, *Orations Against Jews*, 6:2.
10. William Nichols, *Christian Anti-Semitism: A History of Hate* (Northvale: N.J.: Jason Aronson, Inc., 1995), pp. 204, 205. Also see Raul Hilberg's book, *The Destruction of the European Jews* (New York: Harper & Row, 1979), pp. 5ff.
11. Efronymson, "Tertullian's Anti-Judaism," Ph.D. thesis, p. 186.
12. Leonard Swidler, *Biblical Affirmations of Women* (Philadelphia, Pa.: Westminister Press, 1979), p. 343.
13. *Patrologia Graeca* (New York: Adlers Foreign Books) volume 42, col. 740.
14. Swidler, op. cit., p. 346.
15. For an excellent overview of these three levels of honor see Tom Marshall's pamphlet *Explaining Honour and Respect* (Kent, England: Sovereign World, 1991). Distributed in America by Renew Books, Ventura, California.
16. Julian Pitt-Rivers, *The Fate of Schechem; or The Politics of Sex* (New York: Cambridge University Press, 1977).
17. Elizabeth Fernea and Robert Fernea, "A Look Behind the Veil," *Human Nature* magazine, January 1979.
18. Marshall, op. cit., p. 5.
19. James 1:17.
20. Personal conversation in my home with Steven Hawthorne, on the subject of honor. Steve is the coauthor, with Ralph Winter, of *Perspectives on the World Christian Movement*, published by William Carey University, Pasadena, California, and cowriter, with Graham Kendrick, of *Prayerwalking: Praying On-Site with Insight* (Lake Mary, Fla.: Creation House, 1993).
21. Revelation 4:11, *NKJV*.

CHAPTER TWO

The Source of All Honor

*A son honors his father, and a servant his master. Then
if I am a father, where is My honor? And if I am a
master, where is My respect?*
—Malachi 1:6

I once asked a friend what he would do if he saw God. I'll never
forget his answer. He blurted out, "I'd probably throw up." Why
such an extreme reaction? Is God so horrid, so frightening, so
austere that you might lose your dinner with a glimpse of Him?
Not at all. He is stunning. He is breathtaking. He is unswerving-
ly Himself. He is a dread champion, a mighty man of war. His
voice melts mountains. His eyes blaze fire. Prayer leader Joy
Dawson observes, "He is supreme in authority, unquestionable
in sovereignty, magnificent in splendor, dazzling in beauty, and
terrible in wrath."[1] As C. S. Lewis says about Aslan, the Christ
figure in The Chronicles of Narnia, He is not tame.[2]

A TRUE ENCOUNTER
WITH GOD

The Bible is astonishing in its chronicles of an undomesticated
God. Miriam gets leprosy for criticizing Moses. Israel gets forty

years of homelessness for complaining. The earth opens up and swallows Korah and company. Zechariah ends up mute for nine months because of unbelief. One man gets eaten by a lion because he refused to smack a prophet in the face. Uzza steadies the ark and ends up headlining the obituaries.[3] God is not predictable, and He certainly is not safe.

> *A true encounter with God brings you into a new*
> *place from which you can never again return.*
> *You are at that moment and forever*
> *"ruined" for anyone but God.*

In our attempt to put our culture at ease with God, we have reduced Him mostly to a comfortable old shoe. We approach Him with cavalier familiarity. Often, we slop into His presence and congratulate ourselves that we've come. We pray to Him with trifling nasal whines. We give Him paltry sums of time and resources. We know little of the teeth-rattling experience of Isaiah, who saw the Lord sitting on a throne, high and lifted up, His glory filling the room. With smoke rising and posts shaking, Isaiah concludes that his life is over.[4]

Pulitzer Prize author Annie Dillard describes our condition:

> Why do people in churches seem like cheerful, brainless tourists on a packaged tour of the absolute?... On the whole I do not find Christians outside the catacombs sufficiently sensible of conditions. Does anyone have the foggiest idea what sort of power we so blithely invoke? Or, as I suspect, does no one believe a word of it? It is madness to wear velvet hats to church; we should all be wearing crash

helmets; ushers should issue life preservers and signal flares. They should lash us to our pews. For the sleeping God may wake someday and take offence, or the waking God may draw us out to where we can never return.[5]

When given a glimpse of heaven and God's glory, John, on the isle of Patmos, falls at Jesus' feet as dead. Peter cries out much like a leper, "Depart from me; I am an unclean man."[6] Job says, "I have heard of you by the hearing of the ear, but now my eye sees you and I repent in dust and ashes."[7] Elijah sees bone-jarring visions. Daniel faints and is sick for several days. Saul goes blind. Jacob hobbles away with a permanent limp. We know little of the full-throttled race of heart that comes from a true encounter with God.

FOREVER CHANGED

An encounter with God brings you into a new place from which you can never again return. You are at that moment and forever "ruined." When Jesus asked Peter if he was going to leave, Peter says, "Where else can I go?" Not long before, Peter had all the options in the world. He was the sort of man who left himself plenty of room. But then Jesus came into the picture and all of Peter's options flew out the window. Peter, with all his frailties, with his feet alternating positions inside his mouth—good-hearted, rough-hewn, clueless Peter—is forever and completely ruined for anyone but God.

And then, of course, there is Saul. A burr under the saddle of the Early Church, Saul was a relentless hound of hell, never losing the scent of Christians, never losing an opportunity to haul them in for punishment. And then, in one blinding encounter with Jesus on the road to Damascus, Saul is forever and totally ruined for any other purpose than to carry out God's.

An encounter with God produces drastic results.

Consider Moses, spending another have-a-nice-day with the sheep when he saw a peculiar bush aflame but not consumed. He went to look at it and ended up assigned to lead a forty-year field trip with a million-plus preschoolers. (Which goes to prove that an encounter with God can take you places you never really wanted to go.)

One of the dangers in the Church today is that we sometimes create experiences that cause people to think they have met God. We have abbreviated God to such an extent that we invite people to come to Him by simply raising a hand or opening an eye. We are well intentioned in wanting to make God accessible, but I fear in our response to correct shame-based salvation, we have become masters at creating unrepentant conversions. According to George Barna, a large percentage of those who respond to altar calls are not even attending church within eight weeks after the event.[8] Could it be that our present methods of "accepting Jesus" may be keeping people from true repentance?

We have softened all the hard edges and sanded God smooth. We have made Him palatable and reduced Him down to what can sell. In the doing, we have successfully inoculated people from a true life-impacting, vision-changing, future-altering encounter with the living, breathing God.

Some churches tell you they are safe places. And sadly it is true. Of course, when most churches use the word "safe," they mean good things—a place that won't embarrass you; a place of refuge where you don't need to fear the abuse of dysfunctional leadership. But God is not safe. God has never been safe.

Meeting God is, at best, risky business. Jeremiah is cast unceremoniously into a pit for speaking the Word of the Lord. Ezekiel was assigned to do prophetic acts that seemed ludicrous. Jonah may quite possibly have ended up with a lifelong aversion to the sea. Peter ended up crucified upside down.

FINDING OUR FULL DESTINY

If meeting God has such drastic ramifications, why does anyone sane ever put him- or herself in such a vulnerable position? If a true encounter with God draws you out to a place from which you can never return, why not just stay protected in front of the television? Why not just be a nice person who mows his lawn, pays his tithes and taxes and doesn't kick the dog?

The short answer is because our hardwiring was made for God alone. Apart from a true encounter with God, we never truly live. *We were made to know and honor God.* We were not designed to be autonomous creatures operating outside of union with Him. He is our life's breath. We will never be fulfilled apart from knowing the nature and personality of God. We were created to explore Him, to honor Him and to find Him; and we have no ability to fully be ourselves without fully knowing Him.

For lack of knowing God, we abort our full, intended destiny. Symphonies that only could have sprung from a heart inflamed by Him are never composed. Art that could have captured a culture's imagination goes unpainted. Books that could have awakened eternity in a nation's heart are unwritten. Hands that could have healed do not touch. Words that may have affirmed are not spoken. Relationships intended to change the world are never developed. Life goes unlived.

Few people ever discover their full potential and inheritance in God. Part of the reason is that we have worshiped a half-baked God, a benign creature of our own imaginations and not the one true, terrifying yet wonderful God. Instead, we have inherited the God of tradition, the God of other people's perceptions. We have not experienced God for ourselves.

Then the Lord said, "Because this people draw near with their words and honor Me with their lip service, but they

remove their hearts far from Me, and their reverence for
Me consists of tradition learned by rote" (Isa. 29:13).

We have spent centuries seeking to neuter the inherent
potency and unpredictability of God. We want a manageable
God who soothes our wounds and is the ultimate therapeutic.
We do not want a God who is uncontrollable. In our lust for
certitude, we cage Him in tight theologies. We reduce Him to a
warm, fuzzy stress-reducer who helps us cope. The way we present Him these days in print and television, He is not the sort of
God one might die for.

David knew God as tender and full of compassion. He knew
God as a gentle shepherd. He also knew God to be terrifying and
fierce. David wrote of God's arrows being sharp in the heart of
His enemies. He told of how the earth shook, the heavens
dropped and Sinai itself was moved at the presence of God.
David loved a God who had smoke coming out of His nostrils
and fire out of His mouth.

But even David's superlatives blush with inadequacy in
describing God. Terrible in wrath, abounding in mercy, He is, as
international prayer leader David Bryant says, at this very
moment commanding unquestionable complete surrender to
His reign in all nations.[9] He is not a God to trifle with. He is not
the sort of God one can domesticate, and our attempts to do so
dishonor Him.

A. W. Tozer said, "The essence of idolatry is thinking less of
God than who He truly is."[10] In order to truly honor God, we
must know Him. We honor Him by worshiping who He is and
what He is like. We honor Him by knowing His fascinating
nature and personality. We honor God by passionately seeking
Him—panting after Him, yearning for Him, never contenting
ourselves to know just one facet of His character.

We cannot generate a passion on our own for knowing the fullness of God expressed in the person of Jesus Christ. We need to ask the Holy Spirit to give us a lifelong fascination with His character and personality. We were made for Him. He is our heart's true home. We are homeless without Him.

SEEKING THE TREASURE

Have you ever found something so fascinating, so absorbing, that it captured your attention completely? When you absolutely love something, you immerse yourself in it. Dawson Trotman, founder of The Navigators, called this immersion the "expulsive power of a new affection."[11]

Ralph Winter, founder of the U.S. Center for World Missions, once shared how he found out about the power of a new affection. As a young man he loved motorcycles. He would polish and dote on his, taking it apart and putting it back together again just for the sheer joy of it. When he met Roberta, his future wife, he thought that a perfect date was her watching him work on his motorcycle. But she had different ideas. Turns out she didn't even like motorcycles. And here's where the expulsive power of a new affection took over. It wasn't long before Ralph Winter's motorcycle was an abandoned object, forsaken in a corner of the garage.[12]

We honor God by immersing ourselves in Him and considering no detail of His personality as insignificant. People who love God love to talk about Him and exchange notes.[13] They like nothing better than to explore the inner terrain of His heart and mind. They spend their whole lives seeking Him out as treasure.

Jesus compared the kingdom of God to a man who finds a treasure in a field and then sells all he has to buy that field.[14] It's purely speculation, but I wonder if the man in Jesus' story was perhaps actively looking for treasure. I don't think he just walked through the field and stubbed his toe on it. God delights in those who make a diligent search. Those who are willing to sift though field after field till they find gold. God, and the kingdom of heaven, is the treasure worth selling all to obtain. Often we have been content for someone else to buy the field and simply give us visitation rights on Sundays or Wednesdays. God is looking for some passionate people who will seek out His Son.

We honor God by wholeheartedly seeking to possess the treasure of who He is. We need to buy the field, even if it costs us everything. The Father wants to give us the kind of passion and bravery that risks all for the Son. God promised that if we would search for Him with all our hearts, we would find Him.[15] He promised that those who hunger and thirst for righteousness will be filled. He is the One who said to ask and keep on asking. He is the One who said, "I will be found by you."[16]

> Thus says the LORD: "Let not the wise man glory in his wisdom, let not the mighty man glory in his might, nor let the rich man glory in his riches: but let him who glories glory in this, that he understands and knows Me, that I am the LORD, exercising lovingkindness, judgment, and righteousness in the earth. For in these things I delight," says the LORD (Jer. 9:23,24, *NKJV*).

To know God's character and personality is always our greatest need. As God's image bearers, we have to know Him in order to fully understand ourselves. If you've ever gone to a 3-D movie, you know that everything is terribly out of focus until you put on the special 3-D glasses the theater provides. To know God is like putting on those glasses; you can't really see anything clearly apart from Him.

Once we have caught a glimpse of the honor God deserves, we begin to realize the honor of being made in His image. We then have a context for the awesome price Jesus paid at Calvary.

And we hold our breath in wonder that He—God, mind you—invites us to eternal intimacy with Him. It is glory past all imagining. It is an honor from which we will never fully recover.

> *God,*
>
> *You are brilliant! You shine with splendor! You are unfathomable. You are majestic and awesome. All our adjectives falter and blush with inadequacy to describe You. We don't want to deceive ourselves by thinking You are a predictable and manageable God. We don't ever want to cage You. For You are not tame.*
>
> *When it comes to understanding the fullness of who You are, we admit that we are clueless. Yet You honor us with the privilege of knowing You. It is too wonderful for us to comprehend. We long to honor You by passionately seeking You. We want to honor You by knowing all the facets of Your personality and character. We want to honor You with our thoughts, our worship, our everyday lives. Teach us how. Amen.*

SCRIPTURES FOR MEDITATION
Revelation 4:9,11; 5:12,13; 7:12; 19:1,7; 21:24,26

QUESTIONS WORTH ASKING

· Do you ever treat God like "a comfortable old shoe"? Why, or why not?

· Can you think of someone in the Bible who was drawn out into a place from which he or she could never return?

· In what ways do we honor God?

· What is meant by "the expulsive power of a new affection"?

· What are some ways you intend to passionately seek God?

Notes
1. Joy Dawson is quoted in Anne Murchinson, *Praise and Worship on Earth As It Is in Heaven* (Waco, Tex.: Word , 1981), pp. 138, 139.
2. C. S. Lewis, *The Chronicles of Narnia* (New York: Collier Books, a division of Macmillan Publishing Co., 1970).
3. Numbers 12:10, 14:33, 16:31; Luke 1:20; 1 Kings 20:36; 2 Samuel 6:7,8.
4. See Isaiah 6:1.
5. Annie Dillard, *Teaching a Stone to Talk* (New York: Harper & Row, 1982), pp. 40, 41.
6. Luke 5:8.
7. Job 42:5,6, *NKJV.*
8. George Barna, *The Second Coming of the Church* (Waco, Tex.: Word, 1998).
9. David Bryant, *The Hope at Hand* (Grand Rapids, Mich.: Baker Book House, 1995).
10. A. W. Tozer, *The Pursuit of God* (Camp Hill, Pa.: Christian Publications, 1982), n.p.
11. Dr. Ralph Winter, quoting Dawson Trotman, in a talk given in 1993 at a Summer Taste Conference at the U.S. Center for World Missions, Pasadena, California.
12. Ibid.
13. See Malachi 3:16.
14. See Matthew 13:44.
15. See Jeremiah 29:13.
16. Jeremiah 29:14, *NKJV.*

CHAPTER THREE

Honor Given to Man

For You have made him a little lower than the angels,
and You have crowned him with glory and honor.
—Psalm 8:5, *NKJV*

A man in Southern California had a wife who loved garage sales. They were not his idea of fun, but because he was a thoughtful husband he would go treasure hunting with his wife on Saturday mornings. At one sale, he noticed something covered up in a garage, so he lifted up the tarp. Underneath was an old rusty motorcycle.

"How much do you want for this?" he inquired.

"It's not for sale," the owner replied.

"Well, if it was for sale, how much would you want?"

The owner thought for a moment. "I'd take $35."

The motorcycle exchanged hands and sat in the new owner's garage for a very long time.

Finally the man's wife said, "Honey, if you don't do something with that old motorcycle, I'm going to call the thrift store and have them haul it away." So the man went into the garage to assess what it would take to make the rusty thing run.

He wrote down some parts numbers and called Harley-Davidson. There was a long silence on the other end of the phone line. Then the parts department person said he would call back in about an hour.

The motorcycle owner imagined all sorts of scenarios during that hour's wait. *What if a serious crime had been committed by someone riding the bike? What if instead of a call, the FBI came knocking at the door?* Just when he was about to get hives from anxiety, Harley-Davidson called back and asked him to look under the seat and see if anything was written there.

When he reported what he'd found, Harley-Davidson offered the man a six-figure sum for the bike.

What could make a rusty old Harley-Davidson worth that much money? The man's garage-sale motorcycle had been made for Elvis Presley. Its worth was not in itself but for whom it was made.[1]

And so it is with us. We are valuable not in ourselves but because we were made for the pleasure and sheer joy of our great and awesome God. We will never fathom the extent of the honor God has given to man until we realize that God created us for Himself.

This unspeakable honor applies to all men. But our hearts are too shrunken, too unlike God's, to wrap around the truth of this extreme honor to all people. If there is someone particularly unpleasant in your life, you might wonder how in the world that person could be the object of God's affection and attentive love.

GOD SO LOVED THE WORLD THAT HE GAVE

I once heard author and speaker Juan Carlos Ortiz say that God loves man because He made him. Period.[2] God intensely loves the people He has made, and it's important to Him that we understand the value and worth He has given us. After centuries of disobedience and rebellion, you would think He'd give up; but no, God is like the prodigal's father. He never stops longing. He watches attentively, ready to run and embrace us. He takes off

His ring and places it on our finger. God's love is not easily put off. Because God wants to share with us all that He is, He gives us the one thing He alone deserves: He gives us the priceless gift of honor.

If we could isolate and name the various strands of God's DNA (assuming, of course, that God had DNA), one of the markers would be called The God Who Loves, and another would be The God Who Gives. You cannot separate the two concepts. God so loved the world that He *gave*. To Him, loving and giving are never mutually exclusive. By God's very nature He continually loves and He continually gives.

Stroll through ancient mythology, study all the gods and demons who masquerade as deities. You will never find a single one who expresses God's attentive love and continuous giving of Himself. God is not like false gods who are self-absorbed and demand continual sacrifice and misery to be appeased. God wants to give Himself away to those He loves. "No good thing does He withhold from those who walk uprightly" (Ps. 84:11).

Jesus, the supremely honored One of all worlds, heaps honor on those He loves. Likewise, those people who understand honor best, like Him, toss the mantle of their influence, gifts and resources around the shoulders of others. I have an author friend who excels in displaying this characteristic of God. He simply walks into a room, expresses genuine love and honor to the people present and, before you know it, the mantle of honor and favor that God has given him joyfully rests on the shoulders of everyone else. It is an extraordinary grace to observe.

Because God loves us, His actions and speech reflect that love. He does not bellow at us from a distance. He does not disdain our weakness. You will never find God making jokes about our pigpen past. He runs toward us. He wraps a robe around us. He welcomes us with honor, showing us a glimpse of who we can be, not who we are at the present moment. We come to Him clothed in stinking rags and find ourselves suddenly the guest of honor at His party, dressed in His robe, wearing His ring.

His actions toward us are an invitation to do likewise. The Bible is full of instructions on who we should honor. We are to honor God, our parents, elders, our employers, our spouses and those in authority over us.[3] In fact, according to 1 Peter 2:17, we are to honor *all.* God designed human relationships to be nourished and to thrive on honor. This is why all sin is a sin against relationship. What does Satan go after when he wants to destroy our image of God? He goes after our relationships with one another.

In the Ten Commandments, God commanded us to model who He is and what He is like. Our behavior toward one another is to be a sort of living visual aid of how God feels about us.[4] For example, God tells us not to commit adultery because He wants us to model His faithfulness by being faithful to each other. He will never forsake us for someone more desirable. But if we don't have a context for faithfulness in our everyday relationships, we will fail to comprehend the most important relationship of our lives—our relationship with God. He desires our interactions with each other to be mirrors, however imperfect, of His extreme loyalty to us. Children who have never known a father have a difficult time understanding the fatherhood of God. Wives who have been battered, often cannot relate to the tenderness of God as a bridegroom.

God commands us to honor all because He wants us to model His heart and desire toward all He loves. The power of this modeling cannot be underestimated. For want of it, many people and cultures are estranged from God. The lack of Christians who model honor to society is a grave misrepresentation of the heart of God. If we refuse to honor those whom God loves (regardless of their actions), we encourage their alienation and deception, potentially hindering them from knowing the only wise God.[5]

A TRINITY
OF HONOR

God has bestowed on humanity a weighty trinity of honor. He has intentionally dignified man in three astonishing ways. First, He made us in His image. Second, He redeemed us with His blood to prove, as Max Lucado says, "that He would rather die than live without you."[6] Third, He heaps honor on man by inviting him to share His eternal intimacy. This threefold honor toward us is staggering. It is goodness beyond imagining. And it doesn't stop there. The future of those who receive God's kindness is one of increasing, unceasing honor. From the moment of creation to the endless glories of eternity, redeemed man will be the humbled recipient of honor.

GOD HONORS US WITH HIS IMAGE

If you were to buy a franchise of a famous hamburger chain in America, you would automatically be obligated to make hamburgers according to certain specifications. You could not make them out of horsemeat or shape them any way you wanted. You could not have 30 percent fat in your hamburgers one day and 60 percent the next. You couldn't mix soybeans into the meat to make it go farther. You would have strict rules about making your hamburgers because you were selling them under a particular name. Your hamburgers would need to taste exactly like the last hamburger someone bought with that same name, even in another state. They would need to be made "in the image" of the original famous hamburger.

Of course this is a crude comparison, and I am not for a moment comparing you with hamburger, but it underscores a very important point. God did not slop us together. He wasn't simply feeling creative one day and decided to make us on a whim, out of whatever cosmic dust was at hand. When God made man, He chose to make him in His own image.

We do not blow our noses on our national flag or use it for a tablecloth, yet our respect is not for the cloth itself, it is for what it represents. We cannot honor God and dishonor His image bearer.

Man's creation was a tremendous statement of God's esteem.[7] We were crowned with glory and honor by virtue of being fashioned by Him, in His image.[8] We were graced with profound dignity in Eden. Even though Adam and Eve fell through disobedience; even though centuries of broken relationships and heartbreak would follow; even though they were cast out of the Garden, Adam and Eve's inherent honor was not removed from them.

God's image is not erasable from man. To disdain or take one another lightly is to trivialize the image of God. We do not blow our noses on our national flag or use it for a tablecloth. Our respect is not for the cloth itself, it is for what it represents. We cannot honor God and dishonor His image bearer.

You will never meet someone who doesn't have this inherent glory, this extreme honor. Even the most repugnant men of history cannot, by their deeds, obliterate this honor. Even Hitler, Idi Amin and Jeffrey Dahmer—perpetrators of acts so heinous that we can barely comprehend in them any goodness—carried within themselves the value of being made in God's likeness. Surely God wrote them off and rescinded all invitations to partake of His redemption and share His future. Surely their acts invalidated any hope of being valued by God. Yet, by many accounts, serial murderer and cannibal Jeffrey Dahmer gave his heart and life to God prior to being murdered himself in prison.[9] As Corrie ten Boom once said, "There is no pit so deep that the grace of God does not run deeper still."[10] It staggers the mind to think it, but Dahmer could be enjoying the glory and honor of heaven while you are reading this sentence. God's grace and love is that irrepressible.

God did not crown us with honor because we were nice people, or virtuous. He crowned us with *glory* and *honor* (often these words are interchangeable in the Hebrew language) because He made us and intensely loves us, not because of anything we have done in the past or will accomplish in the future.

God Honors Us with His Blood

The God who fills all heavens and more, as Tozer says, "joyfully confined Himself to the virgin's womb."[11] The God whose voice shook the foundations of the deep and whose touch made Mount Sinai smoke and tremble honored His extreme love for us by being with us, taking on the softness of baby skin. Can you imagine that? Many cities take pride that a dignitary, pope or president once visited; and yet, for love of us, God came and camped on our front lawn. God stripped Himself of royal robes and privilege and wrapped Himself gladly in our flesh. And even more amazing, He came for the sole purpose of redeeming us back to God by His blood. Jesus honored us at the highest cost.[12]

Jesus' incarnation was like a giant billboard announcing God's passion for all men. But He did not come to make us feel good. Because He is truth He did not sugarcoat the demands of God. He honored us by being a truth teller.

When Jesus said hard things to the religious people of His day, He was engaging them. He honored them with truth, even when the truth was hard. Calling someone a "whited sepulcher" doesn't sound very honoring, unless you realize that Jesus never diagnosed without offering a cure. If the Pharisees had gone home and wrestled with Jesus' seemingly harsh pronouncements, they could have returned to Him and been healed. A doctor doesn't dishonor a person at the diagnosis of cancer in the person; the cancer is the dishonoring thing. And so it is with our sin. Jesus arrived full of grace, full of truth. We never find in Him grace sacrificed for truth or truth for grace. He is both because God is both. "Mercy and truth have met together. Grim justice and peace have kissed!"[13]

SPEAKING TRUTH AND MERCY

Although Jesus speaks truth very pointedly, and leaves us no room for excuses, His truth can pour healing on our festering wounds. "Neither do I condemn you," He says gently to the woman taken in adultery. "Go and sin no more" (see John 8:1-11). It was the truth about our condition that led Jesus to the Cross. But it was His mercy that absorbed for us the grim realities of our sin. He became sin for us so that we could become the righteousness of God.

Jesus' truth and mercy are an unspeakable measure of our significance to Him. His mercy arouses the eternity hidden in a human heart. On a beach by the sea of Galilee, He said to men with fish guts under their fingernails, "Come, follow Me! I will make you fishers of men!" Even in our undone condition, Jesus calls us into destiny with Him. His words do not malign, they transform. We know His heart and intentions for us are good because He continually honors us with Himself.

Prayer leader Celia McAlpine observes that even Jesus' name points to His passion for us.[14] "You will call His name Jesus for He will save His people from their sins." You cannot even say the name of Jesus without acknowledging the weightiness of His love for us. The blood of God as the value for man's redemption is an inexpressible honor. We "honor all" because God deemed His own blood not too high a price to pay for all mankind.

Shortly after writing this last paragraph I was in a store and noticed a woman wearing not much more than a skinny halter top and shorts. Her stomach was grossly tattooed, and she had several navel rings and various other body piercings. In my opinion the lady was singularly distasteful. As I started to draw back from her, I remembered the honor God had given her in sacrificing Himself for her. I thought of the honor that God had given her by making her in His image and that she, along with me, was invited to eternal intimacy with God. As I thought on these things, I realized I could not disdain her and honor God.

GOD INVITES US TO SHARE HIS FUTURE

To some people, heaven has all the appeal of a trip to the dentist. Mottled wings and hokey harps don't quite capture the vivid reality that awaits us. Some think that life is the real thing, and heaven is sort of the retirement phase. Like we'll play eternal golf until we get bored, and then we'll go fishing.

The truth is that life can't even compare to the real adventure. C. S. Lewis said that we will someday remember the galaxies as an old tale.[15] Scripture is clear. God intends for us to rule and reign with Christ. If we are going to rule and reign, it presupposes that there is something to rule and reign over. We are not told specifically what that will be, except that we will judge angels.[16] But we know that heaven will not be disappointing on any level. If Jesus invites us to rule with Him,[17] you can rest secure that God has something extraordinary in mind.

The whole purpose of history is for God to prepare a suitable bride for His Son. He has invited us to be that bride and share His inheritance and future. God fully intends on making us co-regents with His Son, world without end. Isn't that honor beyond imagining?

By making us in His image, buying us back with His blood and inviting us to share His future and inheritance, God has heaped on man a rich trinity of honor. He has crowned us with dignity, value and significance. Before we ever did a thing, good or bad, honor was extended to us. Because of this high privilege, we are commanded to live a life of honor toward all men.

Envision, in this third millennium, people of honor who are filled with the values of God, loving what He loves, esteeming what He esteems. Will future generations be wooed to the beauty and splendor of Jesus, based on how we love and honor people today? The kingdom of God is a kingdom of honor, and it answers a strong and resounding yes!

Jesus,

You have indeed surrounded us with unspeakable honor. Even angels are puzzled at how You've given to us so freely of Yourself. We cannot take it in. Teach us to live in the joy of having been honored by You so that we give honor to others. Amen.

SCRIPTURES FOR MEDITATION
Psalm 84:11; John 1:14; Romans 5:6,8-10

QUESTIONS WORTH ASKING

· Why does God love us? Why does God love you?
· How has God honored us? What difference does it make?
· How would you define honor?

Notes
1. This is a true story of an acquaintance of John Huffman, pastor of South Coast Fellowship Church,Ventura, California.
2. Juan Carlos Ortiz, (speech presented at a Full Gospel Businessmen's gathering at the Holiday Inn in Ventura, California, 1997).
3. See the following scriptures: God—1 Samuel 2:30, Proverbs 3:9, John 5:23; parents—Exodus 20:12, Deuteronomy 5:16, Mark 10:19; elders—Leviticus 19:32; employers—1 Timothy 6:1; spouses—Ephesians 5:33, 1 Peter 3:7; those in authority over us—1 Peter 2:17.
4. For this concept I am indebted to the wonderful insight of Bible teacher Iverna Tomkins.
5. Of course God always retains His sovereignty in the process of revealing Himself to individuals and cultures. While we can seriously hinder God's intent through dishonor, God can always woo people to Himself by Himself. Writer Flannery O'Connor's in-laws started attending church because "the service was so horrible, [they] knew there must be something else· there to make people come." Quoted by Philip Yancey, *Church: Why Bother?* (Grand Rapids: Zondervan, 1998), p. 21.
6. Max Lucado, *No Wonder They Call Him the Savior* (Portland, Ore.: Multnomah Press, 1986), n.p.
7. See Psalm 8:5.
8. See Genesis 1:27.
9. Philip Yancey, *What's So Amazing About Grace?* (Grand Rapids, Mich.: Zondervan Publishing House, 1997), pp. 95, 96.
10. *The Hiding Place* (Worldwide Pictures, the Billy Graham Association). Filmstrip.
11. A. W. Tozer, *The Attributes of God: A Journey into the Father's Heart* (Camp Hill, Pa.: Christian Publications, 1997), n.p.
12. See John 1:14; Romans 5:6,8.
13. Psalm 85:10, *TLB*.
14. Celia McAlpine, "Praying for the Church in the 10/40 Window," (message given at the 1993 National Lydia Conference in Arrowhead Springs. California). For information on Lydia Prayer Fellowship, contact: Lydia Prayer Fellowship, P.O. Box 4509, Mountain View, CA 94040-9996
15. C. S. Lewis, *God in the Dock and Other Essays* (Grand Rapids, Mich.: Eerdmans, 1994), n.p.
16. See 1 Corinthians 6:3.
17. See 2 Timothy 2:12; Revelation 5:10.

CHAPTER FOUR

Honoring God's Word

My heart stands in awe of Thy words.
—Psalm 119:161

One of my close friends lives on the East Coast. Depending on her hectic schedule, she writes to me fairly often. She's a Jesus lover par excellence and a careful observer of the character and ways of God. Her letters embolden me to love and obey God, and I treasure her words. I place a lot of significance in what she writes because I value her friendship. Her words draw for me a picture of her heart and mind.

The Word of God is a picture of the heart and mind of God. If we would let that truth overtake us, we would be perpetually in awe of the God who speaks to us.

Our first introduction to God, in Genesis, is of Him speaking. He is not silent and brooding. He does not make us guess what He's thinking. He speaks freely, and His words create extraordinary response. Light explodes out of darkness; habitats teem with life when God talks; things that did not exist spring into being. God hung the universe with words. Everything you will ever see, touch or taste had its genesis in a word from God. You exist because God spoke.

The Word of God is a living, breathing journal. It is designed to be an interactive conversation and a field guide into the heart and mind of a person. It is not static. It is not just history. It is not a large assemblage of facts and figures. It is not a lucky rabbit's tail you carry around in your head to ward off demons. And the Word of God is certainly not a weapon to use on those who are not of your persuasion.

The Word of God creates. The Word of God affects destiny. It is like a hammer, like a fire, like a sword.[1] It cleanses. It opens our eyes. It produces liberty. It is forever settled in heaven. It gives understanding to the simple. The Word of God is light. It is pure. It is clean. Every single word of it has been or will be fulfilled. God's Word accomplishes His pleasure. Our pleasure, too, is found in the Word.

There is an old rabbinical story about a holy man who never could get past the wonder of God having spoken. "And God said," he would say with unabashed marvel. "And God said," he would repeat. God speaking to us is indeed a thing so marvelous, so extraordinary, that we should be perpetually in awe. But we often greet the words of God with a stifled yawn.

If we are honest, sometimes the Word is about as captivating to us as instant mashed potatoes. Sometimes it bores us and seems remote and archaic. Instead of feeling awe at the living, breathing, vibrant Word of God, we read out of a sense of duty. Our devotional times with the Word can be stale, cold and cheerless. Sometimes the reason is that we have misconceptions about God.

MISUSE OF THE WORD

If you've grown up in church, you may have painful memories attached to the Word of God. As a child, I heard the Word preached by people incoherent with fury. Veins bulged on foreheads, and I wondered if God could ever speak softly. It wasn't clear to me if God was capable of being pleased.

Some people use God's Word to control people. Others use it to support an evil prejudice. Some hide their emotions behind God's Word. I remember once meeting a pastor who seemed to me like a locker with Scripture bumper stickers all over it. I couldn't reach through the locker to touch the real man inside. Churches split and hearts get torn when people dishonestly use the Word of God to authenticate their offenses. If you have trouble cherishing the Word of God, perhaps it's because you're associating the Word with its misuse.

UNMET EXPECTATIONS

We often don't cherish God's Word because we're disappointed with God. We expected God to heal someone dear to us, and the person died. Or we thought that when God said "Soon" in making a promise, He meant tomorrow.

At seventeen, I lost my love for God's Word under a microscope. The treasure of my childhood became suspect as professors dissected and analyzed God's words into a cramped, airless and irreducibly small box. Some people I know have even deeper pain. A pastor in Canada, as a young boy, would go to recite God's Word to a priest while the priest abused him.

Because God's words are so powerful, Satan (who is a religious spirit) will do anything he can to keep them from you. He will twist them and he will bludgeon you with them until you'd just as soon read anything but them. Satan can even masquerade as the Holy Spirit and use God's Words in a perverted sense to pierce us through with hopelessness of ever pleasing God.

ADDICTED TO LEGALISM

I once heard of a cartoon of a Pharisee doing some street evangelism. He went up to someone and said, "Hi! Have you heard of the 4,982 spiritual laws?" If you have a problem cherishing the Word of God, it is possible that you've encountered a religious spirit. A religious spirit seeks to rob you of hope. It seeks to inoculate you from the Holy Spirit. A religious spirit seeks to deaden you to the vibrant, wholesome wine of God. All it leaves you is a hopeless addiction to rules and regulations. A religious spirit seeks to constrict, to suffocate, to straitjacket you into a state of joylessness. But the very thing a religious spirit seeks to keep you from is your point of deliverance. Jesus said His words are truth. And He said you will know the truth and the truth will set you free.[2]

Our deliverance is in the Word of God. If we are to cherish God's voice we need to seek healing for those places where God's words have been maligned and misrepresented to us. God is more than willing to rinse our minds from the dye of religion and the contorted view it gives us of Him. All we have to do is ask, and keep on asking, with childlike expectancy.

NURTURING THE WORD IN OUR HEARTS

Jesus talked about God's words and our response to them in His parable about the sower.[3] When a sower went out to sow seed, some of it fell by the wayside, and birds swooped down and devoured it. Some seed fell on gravel-like soil. It sprung up for a short time; but the sun scorched it, and it died. Some seed fell among thorns, and the thorns choked it. This sower was probably getting pretty discouraged by now, but thankfully, some seed fell on good soil and produced a crop.

Jesus explained that the seed was the Word of the Kingdom. Seed falling by the wayside represents someone who doesn't understand the Word, and the enemy comes and snatches it away. The gravel-like soil represents someone who receives the

Word gladly; but when hard times come, he gets offended, and the seed dies. The thorns stand for someone who hears the Word, but the cares of the world and the deceitfulness of riches keep him from bearing fruit. The good soil is someone who hears the Word, understands it and obeys it.

God's Word is designed to be heard with our entire personality—our heart, our mind and our will. When we listen with our whole being, we often find ourselves obeying God in fresh, new ways.

Last year a close friend was coming to visit who had never seen our house. I had a lot of months to prepare for her coming. It was a good thing, because I needed them. I worked hard to organize clutter and refinish the dining-room table that was encrusted with seven years of my little son's meals. I reupholstered some chairs. Joey and I planted some grass in the backyard; the old grass had withered from bearing the weight of my son's massive building projects. The amazing thing was how much care needed to go into that hearty grass seed to make it thrive. We fertilized it and watered it five times a day for two weeks. We nursed it into being. We fretted when we missed a watering. And finally, just in time for my friend's arrival, we had lush green grass.

In Jesus' parable, the success of the seed is dependent on certain initial conditions. The Word takes root in nutrient-rich soil. There are some practical ways to enrich the ground of our hearts, but one of the most important is what I call wholehearted listening. Wholehearted listening is not the ultimate cure-all, but when practiced regularly it yields some wonderful fruit.

WHOLEHEARTED LISTENING

A. W. Tozer liked to say, "To understand a Bible text takes an act of the Holy Spirit equal to the act that inspired the text in the first place."[4] We often approach the Word like Sherlock Holmes, looking only for the facts. It is amazing how often we're encouraged to look at the Word of God through the lens of our minds alone. We can get so preoccupied with the facts of the Word that we miss the heart and mind of God altogether. It's good to realize that God's Word is designed to be heard with our entire personality—our heart, our mind and our will. God has designed His Word to engage us on many levels of our being, never just intellectually. When we listen with our whole being, opening up not only our minds but also our emotions and will, we often find ourselves obeying God in fresh, new ways.

Recovering the lost art of biblical meditation and then turning the words of God into prayer is one of the clearest ways to understand the heart and mind of God. When you meditate on God's Word, you take a verse or a portion of a verse and chew it over and over in your mind and spirit, much like a cow chews cud. To switch metaphors a bit, biblical meditation is like letting a verse ripen and open as a flower before the sun. Examine it with your heart from every angle, like a jeweler looks at a jewel from every possible facet.

For example, take the verse, "Let the little children come to me."[5] Take time to let the Holy Spirit unpack that sentence. (Never be in a hurry with God.) Perhaps you might start asking, In what ways do You want the little children to come to You, Lord? How do You want them to come in my neighborhood, my city? What prevents them from coming? Are there ways You want me to be involved in them coming to You?

You might ask God to reveal to you how Jesus felt when He said those words. Was He issuing a dictum to His disciples about who could see Him and who couldn't? Or was He smiling with pleasure, His eyes locked on one child as if they shared a profound secret? Never assume anything when you approach the words of God.

You might meditate on that verse and assume that God has no assignment for you in it, because your spiritual gifts have nothing to do with children. I made that mistake once. Many years ago in Washington, D.C., at a worship conference, a man from Singapore said among many other things that I would have a ministry to children. I scoffed inwardly. I was born forty. I've always loved teaching adults. Children, at that time, were the furthest thing from my mind. I assumed, of course, that he meant children's ministry as we defined it in the church.

Many years later, my husband, Joey, and I produced a children's video on the 10/40 Window[6] that has been well received all over America and translated into several languages. We've gone on to produce children's videos on prayerwalking that have introduced the concept of open-eyed praying to thousands of children.

BIBLICAL MEDITATION

Never try to interpret the words of God through your own limited experience. God sees perfectly. We see in part and understand in part. Never take the words of God lightly, just because they seem impossible. We need to be like Mary, who didn't have the faintest idea of how God was going to accomplish what the angel announced; but she responded with, "Be it done to me according to your word."[7]

Whatever God shows you in His Word, ask Him to help you turn it into prayer. (What He shows you will always agree with the rest of the Bible. The Holy Spirit will never contradict Himself.) You might find yourself, at the Holy Spirit's direction, praying for those who influence children—animators, television programmers, cereal-box designers, school teachers, parents. God could easily have you praying the rest of your life, just from meditating on Matthew 19:14. All you need is the willingness and time for the Holy Spirit to unwrap the gift of His words and teach you how to pray them. Of course, the goal is never how long you pray, it is always how much more of God's heart you know. A simple one-sentence prayer can open a door into the largeness of God. When you pray God's Word back to Him, you come away with an enlarged heart, and your view of God gets enlarged as well.

Biblical meditation allows the Holy Spirit to mentor and nourish your mind and heart as well as your emotions. When you meditate on the Word, you allow the Holy Spirit not only to affect how you think but also how you act. Wholehearted listening is the key to becoming welcoming soil for the potent seed of God's Word to inform all that we do.

One prayer I've been praying for years is that the Holy Spirit will help me tremble at the Word of God. Like Job, I want to esteem His Words more than my necessary food.[8] Jesus said we cannot live by bread alone, but by every word that proceeds from the mouth of God.[9] The Word enlivens us. It wakes our minds and exposes our fallacious thinking. The Word is to be honored as priceless, pure, essential to life. Our destiny is intrinsically interwoven with God's words. We cannot function to full capacity apart from the life-giving, future-directing, thought-provoking Word of God.

The Word will always lead us to the power of God, which is Jesus. A young man who was about to preach his first sermon in a small village church asked an older pastor to attend and critique him. At the conclusion of the service, the young man said, "So, how was the message?"

The older man looked thoughtful for a moment and then replied, "Son, I didn't hear Jesus in it."

"Jesus wasn't in the text," the young preacher said.

"Jesus is in every text, son. Your job is always to find and declare Him."

The heartbreaking fact is that, historically, those who knew the Word of God were often the most unmoved. Who were the authorities of what God had said in Jesus' day? Who were the most unmoved by the presence and power of Jesus? Jesus said, "You search the Scriptures, for in them you think you have eternal life; and these are they which testify of Me."[10] God's words are not simply facts to retain. They are one long arrow, pointing to the passion and power of Christ. We honor God by treasuring His Word.

OUR RESPONSE

Not long ago, I was in a meeting where author Joy Dawson asked each of us to write out a check. She said, "Make it out to 'The maximum glory God can receive from my life,' and leave the amount blank. Let God fill it in. Date it and sign it." We felt holy fear as we solemnly wrote out our intent to obey, regardless of the cost. As I listened to Joy, I thought how little we, as leaders, challenge our people to give God blank checks with their lives.

We have succumbed to the prevalent idea that we can accept Jesus as Savior but not as Lord. We preach an incremental partial revelation of Jesus. It's like salvation on the installment plan. We make the payments really easy at first and hide the actual long-term cost in fine print. "Just come," we say. Then after a few months or years, we slip in, "Oh, by the way, we forgot to mention that Jesus is Lord of your life. He gets to decide everything." Those who actually bow to His rule in every aspect of their lives we consider spiritual giants.

Chuck Colson, in his marvelous book *Loving God*, comes to a simple and startling conclusion that we love God to the extent that we obey Him. Jesus said it quite clearly: "If you love Me, keep my commandments."[11]

Someone once said that the words "No, Lord," were mutually exclusive. You could either say "No" or you could say "Lord," but never both in the same sentence. As A. W. Tozer observes, "The Lord will not save those He cannot command."[12]

I learned the impossibility of saying "No" and "Lord" in the same sentence nine years ago. My biggest challenge of obedience became my biggest blessing. I never wanted to have children. Even as a child I never envisioned myself as a mother. I loved to play with microscopes and chemistry sets. The few dolls I had (which people gave me), I propped up as an audience to preach to. I was a serious child who was forever doing experiments on myself, trying to figure out the cure for the common cold. I was so serious that I used to scoop up handfuls of sand at the beach, burying my face in it as I asked God to give me that many people to lead to Jesus. I had no plans to be a mother; I was going to be a missionary. In my view, children would only complicate things. I planned, among other things, on being a bush pilot.

When I met Joey, I said I wouldn't marry him if he ever wanted children. He swallowed hard, because he loved children, but assured me he wanted to marry me in spite of my stipulation. For fourteen years Joey silently prayed that I would change my mind. Then one Father's Day, a lovely sixteen-year-old friend named Leah pinned a boutonniere on Joey and said he was like a second father to her. Joey was undone. He was overwhelmed with the realization that he wanted it to be his child pinning a boutonniere on him, saying warm, affirming words. So we took one of the hardest walks of my life, and Joey told me his new revelation.

I asked him to simply pray and not pressure me. He did. Finally I realized that I needed to walk off the cliff, so to speak, and simply obey God. I did. It was the hardest thing I've ever done. And that hard-won obedience, that panic-inducing, terrifying obedience, resulted in the birth of an extraordinary little man whom I passionately love.

God commands obedience because He alone has our best interests at heart. He knew what an absolute joy Joel would be to Joey and me. He knew that I would never understand some things without experiencing parenthood. He knew I needed to laugh. (Joel is enormously funny.) He wanted Joel to experience life with us as parents. Obedience was my only alternative if I wanted wholeness.

The reason I've taken up so much space with a personal example is that I think my story is rich with spiritual allegory. We as Christians have not particularly wanted children. We haven't had the passion or patience to deal with all the exhausting attention they demand. We know that new Christians can be a time-consuming bother. They smudge things with their hands, they spill their food, they ask incessant questions. We have to change their diapers. Their growth requires our attentive care. New Christians can seriously interrupt your life.

I have been on several boards of countywide prayer initiatives. We've been blessed with some of the finest of God's men and women, who have shaped and informed our thinking about city-taking strategies. In retrospect, I realize that we accepted one seriously mistaken presupposition—that all Christians in our county desperately want to see new Christians birthed into the kingdom of God. It's sad but true that this has not been a consuming desire. Just as I didn't want natural children ten years ago, before I had Joel, many of us have been disinterested in seeing spiritual children come into the world. We haven't had a heart that says to God, "Give me children or I die." The good news is that today many are turning from their self-indulgent, seminar-hopping, bless-me Christianity and taking radical steps of obedience, asking God to give them a love for the lost, at any cost. If we wept like Hannah, because of our barrenness, God would reward us.

Jesus said, "For the Son of Man has come to save that which was lost."[13] I believe the passion of the third millennium Church will be to see people come to Jesus. We will be less interested in seeking our own comfort and will join the Chief Shepherd who leaves the ninety and nine and goes after the one lost sheep. When we allow the Word of God to penetrate our minds, our wills and our emotions, we will know the passion of God for the lost.

A LIFE PERMEATED BY THE WORD

Several of my friends are authors, and I love watching them when I quote their words back to them. When I do this, it tells them several things. First, it tells them that I've read their books (which is a great compliment to an author; thank you for reading this one). Second, it tells them that their words were significant enough for me to remember them. Third, it tells them that I felt their words were valuable.

When we quote God's Word to Him in prayer, we are saying that we value how He thinks. We are honoring who He is. We have come to think like He thinks, because we have allowed His words full course in our lives.

As author Eugene Peterson observes, "Prayer is everywhere and always, answering speech. It is never initiating speech. *Miqra*, the Hebrew word for Bible, properly means 'calling out'—the calling out of God to us."[14] God's Word is evocative. It elicits response. And the best response of all is prayer.

We honor God by worshiping Him in all the richness of His personality. We honor Him by seeking Him passionately, by treasuring His words and by explicit obedience. Think of it: Whole cultures and their destiny await our engagement with the Word of God!

Word Made Flesh,
  Give me a heart that trembles at Your Word. Let me esteem and honor it and treasure it more than gold. Teach me to listen to Your Word with my mind and heart and soul. I want to know Your Word because I want to know You. I want to obey Your words because they are true, pure and life-giving. I want to love what You love. I want to learn to meditate on Your Word and give it full voice in my life. Grant this, Lord Jesus. Amen.

SCRIPTURES FOR MEDITATION
Read all of Psalm 119.

QUESTIONS WORTH ASKING

· What keeps you from cherishing the Word of God?
· How would you describe wholehearted listening?
· What is biblical meditation?
· In what ways can you honor God's Word?

Notes
  1. See Hebrews 4:12.
  2. See John 8:32.
  3. See Mark 4:3-8.

4. A. W. Tozer, *When He Is Come* (Camp Hill, Penn.: Christian Publications, 1968), p. 32.
5. Matthew 19:14.
6. The 10/40 Window is comprised of the 62-plus countries between the northern latitudes of 10 and 40 degrees, often called the least evangelized countries in the world. *The 10/40 Window for Kids* is a six-minute fast-paced video narrated by children on how to pray for the least evangelized countries on earth. It, as well as *Prayerwalking for Kids: How to Pray for Your City*, is available from Joey and Fawn Parish. For more information, call (805) 987-0064.
7. Luke 1:38.
8. See Job 23:12, *KJV*.
9. See Matthew 4:4.
10. John 5:39, *NKJV*.
11. John 14:15, *NKJV*.
12. A. W. Tozer, *A Treasury of Tozer* (Grand Rapids, Mich.: Baker Book House, 1980), p. 187.
13. Matthew 18:11.
14. Eugene H. Peterson, *Answering God, the Psalms as Tools for Prayer* (San Francisco: Harper & Row, 1989), p. 54.

CHAPTER FIVE

Honor in Prayer

Moreover, as for me, far be it from me that I should sin against the LORD in ceasing to pray for you; but I will teach you the good and the right way.
—1 Samuel 12:23, *NKJV*

Hannah worked with a fellow missionary who practically gave her hives. One day she was complaining to God about this person. As she poured out her heart in a torrent of tears and frustration, she didn't realize she was praying in front of an open window that overlooked a courtyard. Sitting within hearing distance was, you guessed it, the subject of Hannah's prayer. Hannah was mortified and she resolved to never again pray for anyone without the expectation that they might walk into the room in the middle of that prayer. She further resolved that her prayers would be full of honor so that anyone overhearing her would be amazed at what they heard.

The famous missionary to India, Praying Hyde, also had a fellow missionary who was highly irritating to him. One·day, in prayer about the man, Praying Hyde felt the Lord say, "Whoever

touches that man touches the apple of My eye." Praying Hyde
was quick to get the point. God would not allow him to pray
about this man in a spirit of accusation.

A person who honors others prays for them not so much as
they are now but as they could be. When we pray accusing
prayers, we literally turn those prayers into curses. They become
sharp arrows the enemy can thrust into a person's soul—especially a child's. Imagine a child hearing his mother pray this kind
of prayer:

God, help Charlie understand that when he disobeys his
parents he is disobeying God. You know he never obeys.
He is stiff-necked and doesn't listen. I'm at the end of my
rope with this boy. At this rate, I may just have to send
him to reform school. God, do something!

The mother has just handed arrows to the enemy that he can
fire at will on her son. In addition, the child has just listened to
a curse that could become a self-fulfilling prophecy. But what if
she had prayed,

Jesus, I bring you Charlie. You brought him into the
world, and You love him. You have dreams for my
beloved son, and I ask You to fulfill all that is in Your
heart for him. Bless him, Jesus, with a heart that follows
hard after You. Use his leadership skills for Your glory.
Increase Your fame through my son. Let him know Your
love. Make him Your faithful man.

Ah! This mother has just handed to God blessings that He
can use at will!

JESUS' PRAYER LIFE

One of the most touching lines in the New Testament is where Jesus tells Peter that Satan wants to sift him as wheat. Then Jesus says this very striking, tender phrase: "But I have prayed for you, Peter."[1] Imagine Jesus praying like this:

Father, You know these thick disciples You gave me? They're dull about the Kingdom, they rarely understand a thing I say, and Peter, why he's the worst! He only opens his mouth to exchange feet. I'm not sure You're going to be able to establish anything with these guys while I'm gone. But help them, Father. Especially help Peter; Satan is about to broadside him, and he doesn't have a clue.

Can you hear Jesus praying like that? Of course not! But I can imagine Jesus praying for Peter like this:

Father, I love this man. I am about to give My life for him. He has captured My heart. I see his zeal and passion for Me. I see that You are going to smooth many of his rough-hewn edges. You will raise him up to be a powerful leader. He will lead many to You. And Satan is laying a trap for him, a trap he will fall into. Protect him from the voice of accusation. Protect him from the paralysis of analysis. Keep him full of hope. Let him know that My redemption is complete and total. That My love for him is unconditional. Bring him out of this, Father, with a deep compassion for those who have failed. Let him walk with his spirit and head held high in the knowledge that his Redeemer lives. Make him a fisher of men. Give

him the high privilege of feeding Your sheep. You are
able to do exceedingly above all Peter could ask or think.
I commit him to You, Father. Establish him in Your love.

Can you hear Jesus praying like that for *you?*

When we look at the prayer life of Jesus, we see Him praying
wonderful things. In John 17, we find Jesus' most extensive
recorded prayer, one that contains honor in almost every breath.
In this passionate prayer that summarizes Jesus' life, we find the
complete circle of honor. The Father gives honor to Jesus; Jesus
honors the Father and gives honor to His disciples; the disciples
give that honor to Jesus and the Father and those who are yet to
believe on His name. Those who are yet to believe give honor to
the Father, and to Jesus, and to others. And honor flows back to
the Father and begins again. This profound cycle of honor
begins in heaven, comes to earth and ends again in heaven,
thundering through eternity without ceasing.

JESUS HONORS THE FATHER

Jesus' prayer is full of honor. He begins by asking the Father to
glorify Him, not because He is feeling psychologically impoverished, but so that He can glorify the Father. One of the definitions of the word "glory" in the Greek is the word "honor." Jesus
asks the Father to honor Him so that He can honor the Father.
Bringing honor to the Father was Jesus' holy ambition. And God
gets pure pleasure from honoring His Son.

All of history, all civilizations, all of time as we know it can
be summarized in the truth that God is romancing the world to
His Son. It is the Father's pleasure to glorify Jesus. It is Jesus'
pleasure to glorify the Father. Jesus honors (glorifies) the Father
by making Him known. In making Him known, Jesus makes a
way for us to also behold and experience the Father's glory.

Experiencing the glory of the Father is the ultimate possible joy for man.

As pastor and author John Piper observes, "The most precious truth in the Bible is that God's greatest interest is to glorify the wealth of his grace by making sinners happy in him— in HIM!"[2] God's glory is never a private affair. His beauty, His moral excellence, His splendor, His honor increase as we experience Him. And as we experience Him, we, like Jesus, long to increasingly glorify and honor Him. Honoring God becomes our first and last wish and all desire in between.

JESUS HONORS HIS FRIENDS

It goes without saying that the disciples were a tad thick. Even after three years of being with Jesus, they generally didn't get it. Except for a few flashes of anointed inspiration, like when Peter blurted out, "You are the Christ!" most of the time the disciples heard Jesus and scratched their heads. But you don't hear any of that in Jesus' prayer. Jesus honors them in front of the Father. He says: "They have kept Your word. They know You own everything. They have received Your words. They understand. They believe." Jesus seems to be saying, "They get it, Father. They've caught on to what We're up to." I personally think that Jesus was not so much praying the present as He was the future. The truth was, they didn't get it. And if they got some of it, they didn't get much. But you don't hear that from Jesus. He honors them by praying what will become true of them.

This is instructive for us. Jesus models prayer that is future directed and full of faith. He declares what will be true, not simply what is evident. You've heard the old adage, "Any fool can count the seeds in an apple, but only God can count the apples in a seed." This is also quite true of prayer. Anyone can pray the present, but only God can enable us to pray the future. We honor

people when we ask God to give us prayers for them that declare
a future and a hope.

Picture the disciples overhearing Jesus' prayer about them
and then talking to each other. "Did you hear that, Thomas?
Jesus just told the Father that we understand. Jesus said we
believe." Jesus continues, "They are Yours. Keep them in Your
name. Let them be one, even as We are one. Let them have My joy
made full. The world hates them; keep them from the evil one.
Sanctify them in the truth."

"Did you hear that, Peter? Jesus just asked the Father to keep
us from the evil one."

In this recorded prayer in John 17, Jesus doesn't just pray
affirming prayers, He asks the Father for specific things His
disciples will need in the future. We honor each other when we
pray specifically for challenges that are ahead.

JESUS HONORS THOSE YET TO BE BORN

Jesus not only honors the Father and honors His disciples, but
He also honors those of us who are yet to believe. "I don't ask for
these alone but for those who believe in Me also through their
word, that they all may be one; even as you are in Me and I in
Thee, that they may be one in Us; that the world may believe."[3]

Jesus is praying here for many generations that have yet to be
born. And He asks an astonishing thing, that those who are present and those who are yet to come would be one with the Father
and with Him. This is wonder and mystery beyond fathoming.
Jesus prays that we would know the unity He and the Father
know. This is staggering. This is beyond our capacity to understand. Jesus is praying a prayer of immense proportion and
significance. He is honoring us with what means the most to
Him—His oneness with the Father. He is asking the Father to
include us in that relationship.

You can pray with the tenderness of Jesus for those in your city who are yet to believe. You can ask broad and deep things for them. Your prayers do not have to be limited to the present. You can sow prayer into future generations right now, today, if you like.

The power of honor in prayer is that we pray God's heart. We pray His words, His future, His dreams and desires. Our prayers are all about His ability, His plans, His purposes.

When you pray for your children tonight, you can pray not only for them but also for their future children and their children's children. Ask God to make them all passionate worshipers of Jesus. Ask that God's glory and fame would increase through them and their descendants.

The power of honor in prayer is that we pray God's heart. We pray His words, His future, His dreams and desires. Our prayers are all about His ability, His plans, His purposes. The focus of our prayer is not the need, the focus is Him.

HOW WE HONOR GOD

DESCRIBING WHO HE IS

When you hear someone pray who really knows God, you hear him or her talking about God. When you hear someone pray who is just learning, you hear a lot about the present problem.

I remember hearing author J. Sidlow Baxter pray. I couldn't close my eyes; I was transfixed. To hear him pray you would have thought God was standing inches away. And God was glorious in that man's prayers. God was magnificent. He was blazing in glory. In light of His Majesty, it took great effort to remember the problem. I remember thinking that people might even come to God just by listening to J. Sidlow pray.

When you read the psalms, you can listen to the sweet psalmist of Israel pray. He describes God. He talks about the thunder of His voice, how mountains melt at His presence, how God rides on the wings of the wind. David's heart is a torrent of worshipful adjectives. He talks about his problems plenty, but he talks about God more.

ADMITTING WE DON'T KNOW HOW TO PRAY

Adventuresome prayer happens when we admit we don't know how to pray, and we look to God to guide us. Adventuresome prayer is what happens when God is in the driver's seat.

I remember praying with some friends when all of a sudden we felt that we were to pray for Iran. Someone else felt that we were to pray for those who were in prison in Iran. So instead of praying out of our store of knowledge, we prayed what we felt God was telling us to pray. A few days later, we found out that a friend had been falsely imprisoned in an Iranian jail and miraculously had his life spared, right around the time we prayed. Now, most of the time when you hear these kinds of stories, you're tempted to think, *Well, those women were probably intercessors and they probably really hear God, and that wouldn't work for me.* Nonsense! God does not have a special class of people He speaks to more often than others. You don't have to be experienced, seasoned in God, or anything. All you have to be is willing to admit that you don't know how to pray and then listen to the Holy Spirit's impressions.

Don't be surprised if you feel the Holy Spirit impress you to pray about something you'd never expect! One time, prayer leader Joy Dawson felt that God wanted her to pray for people in lighthouses, submarines and bush stations. She obeyed. Quite some time later she related the story to an audience, and someone came up after her message and said, "You know, I worked in the outback, and when I came in to my quarters, the presence of God entered the room and I gave my heart to God." Sure enough, they were able to trace it to the time Joy had been praying. Pascal said that God creates prayer in order to give us the dignity of causality.

ASKING LARGELY

Someone once did a big favor for Alexander the Great. Alexander instructed the man to draw up a bill and present it to the royal treasury. When the treasurer received the bill, he was outraged. He went to Alexander to complain, and Alexander instructed him, "Pay the bill; he honors my wealth by asking so largely." Jesus linked the glory of God to our asking. "Whatever you ask in My name, that I will do, that the Father may be glorified in the Son."[4]

God gets glory from our asking! Jesus said to the woman at the well, "If you knew who I am, you would ask."[5] Jesus equates knowing Him with asking. He also said, "Ask, that your joy might be full."[6]

What's the largest thing you've ever asked of God? I fear we ask for trinkets when He would give us continents. We ask for paltry things when He is willing to give to us largely. Ask God to stretch your ability to ask Him for big things. You might start by asking for your neighborhood or your city. Before long you'll be asking for nations and kings and queens. You can pray with bold confidence when you pray Scripture. Let God amaze you with His willingness. You honor Him by asking largely.

LEAVING OUR BURDENS WITH HIM

I once heard author and Bible teacher Judson Cornwall illustrate a talk by telling of the time when he had the men of his church come early every morning and pray together. They came in all fresh and excited about the day and left to go off to work stoop-shouldered and weary. One day, when he was standing by the door watching them exit, he felt the Lord say, "You know their tiredness is all your fault. You're teaching them to carry the whole world on their shoulders."

Jesus said His yoke is easy and His burden is light. That means that hard yokes and heavy burdens are probably not from God. This includes the yoke of prayer. Yes, God will allow a person to share His grief over an issue, like gender reconciliation. I have seen strong men weep over this issue. But if, after praying, you walk away as heavy as when you started, you're trying to carry what only God can carry. Being yoked with Jesus means that you rest when He rests, and you work when He works. When you get the two confused, you get a chafed neck.

It's comforting to know that we never have to have all the answers. And we can never, in and of ourselves, address every problem in prayer. You simply will feel no desire to address some prayer needs. God has provided people who live and breathe praying for that particular subject. He has wisely distributed varied gifts and interests in His Bride. We never need to be all and know all. There is One who is all, and He is enough.

Jesus,

We echo Your disciples' request: Teach us to pray. Teach us how to honor people with prayer. We want our prayers to be full of blessing. We want to pray Your heart for people, not our own frustration with them. We want to pray with You in the driver's seat, not just out of our own store of knowledge. Teach us to ask largely, because You are honored when we ask. Amen.

SCRIPTURES FOR MEDITATION
John 14:13,14; John 17; Ephesians 1

QUESTIONS WORTH ASKING

· How can prayer sometimes be a curse?
· What are some verses from John 17 that illustrate how Jesus honored His disciples in prayer?
· How does honor pray the future?
· What is the largest thing you've ever asked of God?

Notes
1. Luke 22:32.
2. John Piper, *Desiring God: Confessions of a Christian Hedonist* (Portland, Oreg.: Multnomah, 1989).
3. John 17:20,21.
4. John 14:13.
5. See John 4:10.
6. See John 16:24.

CHAPTER SIX

Honoring the Bride

Come, I will show you the bride, the Lamb's wife.
—Revelation 21:9, *NKJV*

I was in Atlanta, leading the worship for a national Lydia Prayer Fellowship conference. It was the first session, and the microphones were open for repentance. If God was prompting anyone in the building to repent, they were invited to address the crowd. As I sat at the piano, which was lower than the stage, my eye caught sight of an elderly woman's leg as she slowly and painfully ascended the steps to the microphone. I don't remember what she said, it was the sight of her leg that caught the eye of my heart.

Her legs were stout and weathered, rising from her shoes like tree trunks in pots too small. They had known greater days of glory. But as I looked at her legs, I was awash with love for the beauty of Christ's Bride. I sat at the piano completely and unutterably undone.

I was in California when the beauty of Christ's Bride again caught my eye. I was with sixty reconciliation leaders from around the world. We had gathered for three days, simply to seek the Lord. As my eyes swept around the room, looking into the faces of my Jewish, Maori, Swiss, African, Australian and British brothers and sisters, I was amazed at Jesus' restraint to not come immediately and consummate this brilliant, surprising marriage. In this room were strong visionary leaders, men and women who could have preceded themselves into the room. But here they were, humbled and graced by God, preferring one another in love. It was a sight too holy to adequately describe. My heart could barely take it in. *So this is what You died for, Jesus,* I thought to myself. *So this is what You live to honor.*

The New Testament is clear; the magnificent obsession of Jesus is to honor His Bride. He loves her; He gave Himself for her; He fully plans on spending the rest of His life with her. Jesus lives and breathes honoring His Bride. All history, all civilizations, all of time can be compressed into this one holy ambition. In desiring a bride for His Son, God has romanced all the peoples of the world, throughout history, with a strong wooing. And she is magnificent.

While some may look at the politics and scaffolding of the institutional church and smirk at its frail, ego-driven hypocrisy,[1] others see the splendor of Maoris, Africans, Native Americans, the Sammi, the Chinese and the Jews, who are joining a countless throng of people from many nations to worship the Lamb with humility and wholehearted adoration. This Bride is stunning. And she is getting more beautiful by the day.

GOD'S CHOICE OF A BRIDE

Where did this Bride come from? She originated in the mind and heart of God. She was the ultimate purpose for creation. A. W. Tozer observes a parallel between Adam and Jesus.[2] Adam named all the animals and was disappointed to not find some-

one of the same nature as himself. There was no animal worthy
of Adam, no animal who could fully meet him. God, realizing
Adam's need, put him to sleep and fashioned a bride named
Eve, out of Adam's side. Jesus, the second Adam, also could not
find one among the daughters of men who was of the same
nature as Himself. Jesus found no one worthy. So God, on the
cross, opened Jesus' side. Out from His side flowed not a rib,
but water and blood. From that water and blood God is washing, cleansing and preparing a Bride worthy of Jesus. Out of
Jesus' side flowed a pure, holy Bride without spot or wrinkle
and taken from every tribe and tongue. Out of Christ's side
flowed a people whom God would gift to His Son and to each
other—a people rich with the honor of having been loved by
Love itself.

This Bride is staggering. I am not ashamed to tell you, I love
her. I have seen her beauty in a man named Sam Chapman, a
large gentle man who can make your heart race at the fierce jealousy of your God against His enemies. When Sam does the
Maori war dance, the Haka, something inside your spirit gets
rearranged and is never quite the same.

My heart has been enlarged as I've watched the tender
worship of the Sammi of Norway.[3] I have seen the Bride's beauty in the quiet intercession of my Canadian Cree friend, Carol,
who counsels alcoholics and drug addicts. The blood of Jesus
was well spent in obtaining this glorious woman.

When Jesus looks at His Bride, He will never regret the price
He paid.[4]

I am new to this appreciation of Christ's stunning Bride.
Someone once said that cynicism is the lazy habit of a thinking
mind. And I have been lazy. During the seventies, in Bible
college, my friends and I sang these words to the tune of
"Onward Christian Solders":

Like a mighty tortoise moves the church of God;
Brothers we are treading, where we've often trod.
We are all divided, not one body we;
Having different doctrines, not much charity.

When we criticize the Church, we are criticizing
something Jesus adores and spilled His blood for.
It is His own precious possession.

I often quoted the pun that the church is like Noah's ark. It stinks but it's the only thing afloat. You see, it's easy to scoff at something you don't understand. It's easy to criticize the thing that has wounded you. But when we criticize the Church, we are criticizing something Jesus adores and spilled His blood for. It is His own precious possession.

In my early cynical days at Bible college, I made a mistake that many make. I mistook the chrysalis for the butterfly. The gorgeous Bride of Christ is hidden inside a necessary wrapping that often bears little resemblance to her true image. The institution is mere scaffolding; the people inside are the true building. The institution has often historically misrepresented God's heart to the world. In the lyrics of a song by Gloria Gaither, the church has been "gold-plated, draped in purple and encrusted with jewels, but God has always had a people."[5]

A few weeks ago, a friend said something that went straight to the marrow of my bones. He said quietly and without fanfare, "It's easy to mock what you haven't given your life for." As I looked at this gifted pastor, I realized he had and was giving his life for his sheep in Washington, D.C. As a man of many talents, he could have been anything he wanted. But instead of climbing to the top of academia, he was quietly giving his life away for the Bride.

GOD HAS ALWAYS HAD A PEOPLE

Walk through any period of history and you will find lovers of Jesus who are too astonishing for words. You don't have to look far. There is a long line of men and women of whom the world was not worthy—people who loved with fierce strength and who brought joy and blessing to the wounds of many.

I think of Jim Elliot, the martyred missionary who gave his life for the Auca Indians of Ecuador. When you read an entry in Jim's journal it feels like you're stumbling into an intimate moment between two lovers. You feel like you need to shade your eyes from the passion of this man's heart toward God.

> Oh the fullness, pleasure, sheer excitement of knowing God on earth. I care not if I ever raise my voice again for Him, if only I may love Him, please Him. Mayhap in mercy, He shall give me a host of children that I may lead through the vast star fields, to explore His delicacies, whose finger-ends set them to burning. But if not, if only I may see Him, touch His garments, and smile into my Lover's eyes—ah, then, not stars, nor children shall matter—only Himself.[6]

The Bride of Christ is gorgeous. She is not limited to any age, gender, tribe or tongue. Anywhere in the world you go, she is there, passionately loving her Bridegroom. You will find her in the slums of Calcutta, tenderly nursing maggot-infested bodies. You will find her in Brazil, feeding street children. You will find her in Siberia, braving uranium poisoning, joyfully telling others about her Bridegroom. You will find her gently wiping the face of those dying of AIDS in Los Angeles. You will find her in Rwanda. She is everywhere, and she is beautiful.

Recently I met Dr. Rhainnon Lloyd, a Welsh psychiatrist who works among the Hutus and Tutsis of Rwanda. Dr. Lloyd helps these two tribes deal with the unfathomable tragedies of their recent civil war. Dr. Lloyd gives three-day workshops on forgiveness and reconciliation. In a Rwandan culture that does not smile on the showing of emotion, she has the Hutus and Tutsis tell their stories and then write them out. At the final session, with strong crying and expressions of forgiveness, many nail their stories to a large wooden cross on the floor.

I had heard stories of Dr. Lloyd before meeting her. In my mind she had taken on folk-hero status. But I was wholly unprepared for who she actually is—a humble, middle-aged woman, absolutely brimming from every pore with love for her God and a passion for Africa. Dr. Lloyd loves the people she works with. They are her friends. She is no cold clinician in a white smock, mouthing reconciliation. She is warm, alive, vibrant with creativity. Her face holds the ultimate compliment to a life well lived— she has smile wrinkles. Yes, God has always had a people.

See the unspeakable attractiveness of the Bride in the Chinese house church pastor who was sentenced by his government to work many hours a day in a sewage pit that was chest high. As he waded through the refuse, the man would sing love songs to God. His favorite song was "In the Garden."

> I come to the garden alone,
>
> While the dew is still on the roses;
>
> And the voice I hear, falling on my ear,

The Son of God discloses.

And He walks with me, and He talks with me,

And He tells me I am His own;

And the joy we share as we tarry there,

None other has ever known.[7]

He later recounted that his times of worship as he worked in the raw sewage were so sweet, he could often smell flowers.

Most of the gorgeous people who make up the Bride will never appear in books or magazines. They will not have prominent ministries or be considered God's voice to their generation. But they are the complete objects of Jesus' affection. They are beautiful and "terrible as an army with banner."[8] They are mothers of young preschoolers, who faithfully love their children and do the hard, everyday, ordinary stuff to help them grow; they are elderly grandmothers who sit and "pray in" the next generation; they are young men who turn a deaf ear to the seductive voices surrounding them and live pure, holy, God-focused lives; they are grown men who spend their lives serving and loving what God loves.

THE ONE WHO LOVES AND ADORNS US

The Bride is unspeakably beautiful because of who loves her. In the book of Ephesians, Paul's words tell us that Jesus nourishes and cherishes the Bride. In the Song of Solomon, we hear the emotive love of Christ for His Bride. "You have made my heart beat faster, my sister, my bride; you have made my heart beat faster with a single glance of your eyes."[9]

This passionate love of Jesus, unlike any earthly love, will not ebb and flow like the tide. Romans 8:38 tells us that absolutely nothing in hell or heaven will be able to separate us from His love. Not stinking death, not the daily ordinariness of life, not angels, not demons, nothing in the present or the future. Nothing. Not time nor space. No circumstance or personality, godly or devilish, will be able to keep us from His love. Jesus' love for His Bride is completely secure. It is unconditional. It is unwavering.

The Bride is not beautiful because of some intrinsic goodness in her. She is not stunning because she happened to be born more beautiful than the rest. She is beautiful because she has allowed the Holy Spirit of God to transform her. She has allowed the Spirit of God to adorn her and make her as a bride prepared for her husband. The thorough work of the convicting power of the Holy Spirit has been allowed full voice. She, as Esther many centuries before, has submitted herself to much cleansing and preparation before she walks toward the extended scepter of her King.

As I have met people on various continents and enjoyed the splendor of the Bride of Christ, I've noticed something that is universally true. Those who continue to welcome the Holy Spirit's conviction into their lives become increasingly more like Christ. And those who don't, become frozen in time. Although they are redeemed, their beauty does not increase.

Esther realized that having beauty was not enough. She listened to Mordecai and submitted to the preparations suggested by the King's eunuch, Hegai.

> Now when the turn of Esther, the daughter of Abihail the uncle of Mordecai who taken her as his daughter, came to go into the king, she did not request anything except what Hegai, the king's eunuch who was in charge of the women, advised. And Esther found favor in the eyes of all who saw her (Esther 2:15).

The text is clear that the other young women could take anything they chose out of the wardrobe before they went into King Ahasuerus, but Esther let another pick her garment.

The beauty of Christ's Bride is that another, the Holy Spirit, dresses her. She does not rely on her own taste, style or fashion. She is beautiful because Beauty itself adorns her.

Jesus doesn't have a prenuptial agreement with His Bride-to-be. He didn't write up a contract that says certain portions of His wealth will not become hers. He did not say that certain accounts are off limits, that certain trusts are to remain solely for His use. No. He gives all of Himself to His Bride, without reservation. "And to know the love of God which passes knowledge, that you might be filled with all the fullness of God."[10] And again, just in case we missed it, "From his fullness we have all received, grace upon grace."[11]

Jesus gives everything to the Bride—His wealth, His inheritance, His honor. All that Jesus has and is, He has joyfully given to His Bride. We do well to honor her, as she is the supreme object of Jesus' affection.

Bridegroom,

Your Bride is beautiful—beautiful to You, and beautiful to us. She really is quite stunning. Everywhere we go, we see her, and she is getting more beautiful by the day. Teach us to honor her. Let us speak softly to her. Wash away all the cynicism and division in our minds about her. We want to see her as You do, for we are a part of her. Amen.

SCRIPTURES FOR MEDITATION
Esther 2:15; Anywhere in Song of Solomon; Ephesians 3:17-19

QUESTIONS WORTH ASKING

· What are some ways people dishonor the Bride of Christ with their speech?

· Why should we honor what Christ honors?

· Why is Jesus so deeply in love with His Bride?

· What are some ways you could experience for yourself, and then share with others, the honor of being the Bride?

Notes

1. I freely acknowledge that the history of the Church is filled with contradiction. Ray Stedman, in the book *Body Life* (Regal Books, Ventura, Calif.: 1972), talks of two churches: "Both are religious but one is selfish, power-hungry, cruel and devilish. The other is strong, loving, forgiving and godly. One has fomented human hatred and caused society to erupt in continual bloody conflicts, all done in the name of God and religion. The other has healed human hurt, broken down barriers between race and class, and delivered men and women everywhere from fear, guilt, shame and ignorance."

The Church in history has not always represented the personality and character of God in its actions. Former Senate Chaplain Richard Halverson has been credited with saying that Christianity began as a fellowship centered around the person of Jesus; it went to Rome and became an institution; it went to Greece and became a philosophy; it came to America and became an enterprise. But God has always had a people. Since Calvary, Jesus has always had a stunning Bride. When I talk about honoring the Bride, I am not saying there is no room for honest assessment of the Church. When we honor the Bride, because we realize the price Jesus paid for her, we are not saying she is faultless. As prayer leader Celia McAlpine told me during a conversation, "It is a brilliant contradiction; Jesus is completely subjective and completely objective about His Bride." He is madly in love with her, and He knows perfectly well all her faults. Elton Trueblood says, "We should pay attention to those who love her (the Church) so deeply that they want her to achieve her true character. When a Christian expresses sadness about the Church, it is always the sadness of a lover. He knows there have been great periods and, consequently, he is not willing to settle for anything less than those in his own time." (Elton Trueblood, *The Incendiary Fellowship* (New York: Harper & Row, 1967), p. 100.

2. A. W. Tozer, *Rust, Rot or Revival* (Camp Hill, Penn.: Christian Publications, 1992), pp. 128, 129.

3. The Sammi are an indigenous people of Norway, Sweden, Russia and Finland. They were formerly called Laplanders.

4. See Isaiah 53:11.

5. William J. and Gloria Gaither, "The Church Triumphant," © 1973, Gaither Music Management, Alexandria, Indiana. Used by permission.

6. Elisabeth Elliot, *Shadow of the Almighty* (Grand Rapids: Zondervan, 1958), p. 142.

7. C. Austin Miles, "In the Garden," 1912, by Hall-Mack Co. Public domain.

8. Song of Solomon 6:4,10.

9. Song of Solomon 4:9.

10. Ephesians 3:19, *NKJV*.

11. John 1:16, *RSV*.

CHAPTER SEVEN

Honoring Diverse Cultures

It takes a whole world to understand a whole Christ...
—Kenneth Cragg[1]

I was convinced I was scheduled for a divine encounter on this flight. It didn't take long, however, to discover that I was invisible to my seatmate. Through his newspaper he emitted short waves of don't-even-try-to-make-conversation radar. My confidence was eroding fast. It's particularly difficult to have a divine encounter when you don't exist.

On the connecting flight out of Phoenix, I climbed aboard an older plane, but my hope swiftly evaporated as I scanned the aisle numbers. I had assumed that since nothing had happened on the beginning leg of my journey, this must be the flight where I was supposed to meet someone God wanted me to talk to. It became obvious within moments that I had the scene right but the roles reversed. I was seconds away from meeting a stranger who would radically challenge most of my long-held, well-established, of-course-they're-correct presuppositions.

I found my seat, thrust my luggage overhead and spied a Middle Eastern man. We silently regarded each other. *Perhaps this is the man,* I thought. I remembered that a friend who had lived in Beirut told me that as a woman you need to be careful not to look Arab men directly in the eye, as it is considered seductive. I kept my gaze humbly pinned to the floor. Finally, he spoke.

"Are you on your way to Colorado Springs?"

"Yes."

"Are you staying at the Radisson?"

I answered in the affirmative.

"Are you going to the conference?"

Again the answer was yes. It's hard to have a serious conversation with your gaze on the ground and your speech restricted to monosyllables.

Then this middle-aged man said, "I hate conferences."

"I do, too," I replied.

Ah! We finally had something in common. Mutual dislike can go a long way toward friendship. *A divine encounter might be about to happen after all,* I thought.

I asked him to tell me his story. Over the rumbling noise of the engines, with my gaze still fastened to the floor, he unfolded an amazing tale. He was from a prominent Middle Eastern family and had come to love and trust Christ. I asked how his family had responded to his conversion, and he proceeded to loosen his tie and pull down his white shirt collar to show me a large scar over his jugular vein. Immediately this man had my full attention. How many times do you get to meet a living martyr? With just one gesture he had instant credibility, but his authority proved to be short-lived.

I mentioned that I was interested in developing some television programs for women in the Muslim world that could be beamed in by satellite. When I innocently asked for his counsel, his words erupted like lava filling the aisles and oozing up onto my seat. "You American Christians are impossible! You always want to beam things in. You have no idea of the value of sitting across the table, having coffee and getting to know my people up close! You don't understand the slightest thing about honoring my people or their culture!"

I'd obviously touched a nerve. As he proceeded to vent his geyserlike frustration, challenging everything I'd ever thought about Middle Eastern eschatology and politics, I began to pack him politely into a box I reserved for well-intentioned but very wrong brothers. I was sure he was simply an inflamed zealot. While I didn't doubt his love for God, I doubted everything else he stood for.

God has purposely placed aspects of His own character and personality in each culture so that we can come to understand and enjoy who He is more completely as we understand and enjoy one another.

As I self-righteously listened, a curious thing began to happen; the more he talked, the more I found myself loving him. My head and heart plunged into a boisterous argument. My head vehemently disagreed with his politics, while my heart resonated strongly with the truth of his observations.[2]

I had to admit he was right. We do want to "beam" things in to people. As Americans in ministry, we do tend to be long on technology and short on relationship. We've been artless when it comes to sitting down with people and hearing their stories. We haven't modeled the God who enjoys people simply because He made them. We don't understand honor, even in our own culture, let alone a Middle Eastern context.

In our zeal for conversions, God's highest and best creations sometimes get marked simply as potential converts—scalps on our spiritual belts. People whom God highly prizes have become statistics to validate our ministries. They make good fund-raising stories, propping up fragile kingdoms and frail egos.

This Arab gentleman was right. We often do think that sitting down and having coffee together is a waste of time. We aren't willing to spend years getting to know someone for the sheer joy of knowing them. While there are people who are wonderful exceptions to this way of relating, most of us want immediate results, preferably in the form of conversions to Christianity. Our interest in people only extends to them while they are potential converts.

My newfound friend talked nonstop till we arrived at our destination. I realized that I probably wouldn't be producing television for the Middle East, after all. Like many before me, I had mistakenly assumed that because I knew the Word and the need and had the technology, I was prepared and authorized to speak to another culture.

I found that I needed to reevaluate my ideology. It's humbling to have all your well-fed presuppositions sloughed off in a heap when you've only known someone for less than an hour. But there I was, having a divine encounter of the very worst kind. Like Job, my hand was "upon my mouth."

THE DISTINCTIVE
GIFTS OF EACH CULTURE

One of the ways we honor God is by honoring the beauty of Him and the gifts He has placed in other cultures. When we do this, we acknowledge that our culture is not sufficient in and of itself to fully experience or express God. He has purposely placed aspects of His own character and personality in each culture so that we can come to understand and enjoy who He is more completely as we understand and enjoy one another.

The apostle Paul said that we are many members but one body.[3] A whole body cannot be made up of only an eye or a tongue. Our body parts could get in an argument over who's the most important or the most useful, but the whole argument would be absurd. We're incomplete without each other. And so it is with culture.

When we enjoy God's gifts in each other, we honor Him, the Grand Gift Giver. We honor God by recognizing and responding to His revelations of Himself in every culture.

THE BRITISH ARE COMING!

There was a time not that long ago, when the sun never set on the British Empire. God gifted the English with particular vision and courage to thrive in a cross-cultural context. They had a particular talent for leadership and for creating a replica of their own culture in wide-ranging environments. I believe this distinctive ability to establish themselves throughout the earth was intended for them to fill the earth with the knowledge of the glory of God.

The British have gifts of administration and organization. They tend to be builders. They love to improve things. They enjoy a challenge. They have blessed the world with hospitals and orphanages and education. While these gifts, in some cases, were misused to dominate and conquer, the gifts themselves were from God, the giver of every good and perfect gift.[4] As in any culture, pride and mammon have sought the starring roles. But I believe England's best days are still ahead. God is doing a rare and wonderful thing there. He is gifting them with strength and humility to bestow honor on the peoples of the earth. They have given the world priceless gifts of leadership and organization, and we owe them honor.

British prayer leaders have been seen lately all over the world, repenting for those parts of their history that were unjust. One man wept before a gathering of Native Americans, confessing that his family had made the English barrels containing the alcohol that would prove so destructive to the Native American community.

Recently a team of British prayer leaders went through Australia, asking forgiveness for past injustices done by the British. One aboriginal boy, whose grandfather had been blinded by atomic testing by the British, went up to one of the prayer leaders and said, "Have you come to tell my grandfather sorry?"

"Yes," the man replied.

"Okay, then you can be my friend."

THE GIFTS OF THE JEWS

God has given the Jews a very central place of honor, above all nations.[5] Jews are to be celebrated and acknowledged as having given the world unspeakable gifts.[6] As author Thomas Cahill points out, our concepts of linear progression come from the Jews. Prior to this, mankind thought of life in terms of a circle. Life was a wheel, and you didn't have much control over the outcome. Fate dictated all, and everyone was fairly resigned to the fact that they could not change much. Epidemics were fate; being poor was fate; being at the bottom of the food chain, economically speaking, was again fate.

Then Abraham came along and gave the world the gift of a processive view.[7] Life is a journey with a beginning, middle and end.[8] His story showed us that we can affect how the story unfolds. We have the dignity of causality. We can leave the familiar, same ol' lamo existence in Haran and journey into an unknown land. We aren't even sure of the name of our destination, but God says, "It's a land I'll show you."

The enormous worth of this gift of a processive view versus a circular view cannot be overstated. It makes science and discovery possible. It means that man is significant and can effect change. The Jews also gave the world the concept of justice. The verse in Isaiah 33:22, which says, "For the Lord is our judge, the Lord is our lawgiver, the Lord is our king," provides the basis for the evolution of our concepts of three branches of government—presidential, judicial and legislative. It was the Jews who gave us the concept of justice for the poor and needy. ·

As the Early Church grew, and more and more Gentiles became believers, the tail began to wag the dog. We dishonored our Jewish brothers and sisters and said that if they wanted to be *real* Christians, they would abandon their Jewishness. We forgot that we were honored to be grafted into the branch. Instead we uprooted the whole tree.

We did this calamitous thing through the arrogant error of extreme replacement theology. This teaching basically said that God had disinherited the Jews, nullifying His promises, and had given those promises to the Gentile Church instead. Extreme replacement theology created a seedbed for anti-Semitism in the Church. This gave birth to devilish practice and thought. For centuries, Jews have seen Christians as their primary persecutors. The Inquisition, the Crusades, the pogroms in Europe—history is full of hate perpetrated on the Jews in the name of Christ.

We are now living in a time when God is awakening us to the honor due our elder brothers. I have watched men and women weeping in repentance for our history of hate toward the Jews. God is pulling back the covers of history, and we are seeing our sin as never before. In addition, we are receiving soft hearts to walk in humility and to honor God's chosen, our elder brothers.

God is honoring Jews with a resurrection of their own Jewishness. According to an article in *Christianity Today*,[9] in 1967, before the Jewish people regained control of Jerusalem, there was not a single Jewish messianic congregation in the world and only several thousand messianic Jews worldwide. Now, over 350 messianic congregations—50 in Israel alone—dot the globe. These congregations see their role as twofold: to help Jews understand Jesus as their Messiah and to help the Christian Church understand her Jewish roots.

As Christians, we owe our messianic Jewish brothers a great debt. They are the root to which we have been grafted. To them belong the adoption as sons and the glory and the covenants. To them belong the giving of the Law and the Temple service and the promises. They are the fathers.[10]

LETTING OTHER CULTURES BE WHO THEY ARE

One of the most amazing facets of how God honors us is that Jesus chose to live among us. Jesus lived as a first-century Palestinian. He spoke Aramaic. He lived like other boys in His neighborhood. He apparently was so much like everyone else that on the night before the Crucifixion, Judas had to single Him out with a kiss to identify Him. The Word became flesh and dwelt among us. He lived like us.

Many years ago, Ralph Winter, the director of the U.S. Center for World Missions, made the observation that where missions had imposed a foreign culture on a people, within the second generation, the converts were not self-propagating. There was no strong indigenous missionary movement. However, in missions that tried to adapt to the culture around them, the second generation of converts were Great Commission Christians and had strong indigenous missionary activity.[11]

THE TOBA PEOPLE

In 1950, Albert and Lois Buckwalter went to indigenous tribal groups in northern Argentina. They translated the entire New Testament into the Toba, Mocovi and Pilanga languages. They entered Argentina fully intent on following the traditional Mennonite Mission pattern,[12] which meant building a mission compound, church building, school clinic, carpentry shop, store and so on. But then they realized that "the Toba people weren't really interested in hearing us. In fact, it seemed they would not become Mennonite in even 200 years."[13]

A Christian anthropologist-linguist couple opened their eyes to the problem. The Toba people were developing a culturally appropriate response to the Christian gospel but were hiding it from the Buckwalters, fearing they would leave. The Toba, it seemed, were holding unauthorized meetings in their own language in one of the Mennonite churches. They were worshiping with their own chosen leaders. Albert and Lois, under biting criticism, took a bold leap of faith. They announced that they were no longer in charge of the Toba churches. They would continue to visit and bring the Word of God, but only at the request of the Toba people themselves.

The Toba people turned to Jesus Christ to heal them, body and soul. They lost their faith in their native healers, in the traditional taboo system and in the spirits they believed had healed them in the past.

The Buckwalters write of their forty years with the Toba,

It cemented into our souls the reality of a God with far greater power and love than we could have known without having experienced it among the indigenous Christians of the Argentine Chaco. It helped us understand that every people has its own history, its own way of coping with reality, and that any new concept has to be received and reinterpreted in light of its own experience. It is impossible for people to respond to God authentically in any way other than their own. When we are too easily convinced of our superior knowledge of how the Christian faith should be expressed, we rob ourselves—ourselves, mind you—of seeing the glory of God in its fullness.[14]

The Buckwalters refused to impose their own culture and way of doing things on the indigenous Christians of the Argentine Chaco. And for their boldness they saw the birth of a healthy Church.

HONORING OUR OWN CULTURE

Last year I was in Jerusalem, having breakfast with a messianic Jewish leader. He talked about the people who come to Israel and completely disavow their own culture. He considers them Jewish wannabes. Every culture has them. People who see only the good of their adopted culture and only the bad of their own. I have seen white people want to be black, and black white. I've seen whites want to be Native American. As the Holy Spirit gently reveals much of Occidental Western history that has brought dishonor to other cultures, it is easy to become uneasy about being of European ancestry. But every culture has aspects that point to God Himself. And every culture has aspects that are demonic.

When we honor God by honoring and celebrating other cultures, we honor Him when we celebrate our own culture as well. Then we are celebrating in truth. Then we are being honest about the fact that some things in other cultures are irritating. If you're living in a culture other than your own, and you haven't experienced any cultural irritants, you're probably in deception or in deep cultural infatuation.

We do not honor another culture by idolizing it and disavowing our own. We cannot truly honor something unless we do it in truth. I see this honesty becoming increasingly vital as we move together into the third millennium. Only the kingdom of God is a perfect culture. We, on the other hand, are all fragile earthenware. We have victories and triumphs to celebrate in our history, and we have sin for which we gladly repent. Our universal story is that we all desperately need God.

I have an insightful friend who once asked God why He created the races. My friend is white, and she is the mother of two gorgeous African-American boys. Her heart was broken at the treatment they routinely received because of their skin color. "Why did you create us so different?" she asked God. Then she heard Him gently answer, "So you could never pretend you knew how to love."

When we honor other cultures, we need to admit that we do not know how to love. We are by nature people who feel most comfortable around people like us. As we ask for the love of God to enlarge our hearts, desiring to love with His love, we find our circle of inclusion ever widening. When we honor other cultures, we must continually ask God to let us see with His eyes and not our own. We must seek His love to continually enlarge our hearts to love others.

Lord Jesus,

Your Bride is stunning! Thank You for including us. We treasure Your marvelous multicolored wisdom. Teach us how to listen to each other's stories and songs. Let us give place to each other. We want to find more of You in each other. Culture is a treasure map, and You are the treasure. You are the desire of the nations. You are the desire of our hearts. Amen.

SCRIPTURES FOR MEDITATION
Ephesians 3:10; Revelation 5:9; 7:9

QUESTIONS WORTH ASKING

· What are the distinctive gifts of your culture?
· Why does God take pleasure in the diversity of His people?
· Why should our worship on earth reflect what it will be like in heaven?
· How can we honor other cultures by praying for them?
· This week, ask God for one specific way you could apply what He is showing you on this subject. How will you put it into practice?

Notes

1. Kenneth Cragg, *The Call of the Minaret* (London: Oxford University Press, 1952), p. 183.
2. This conversation forever changed my view of God's heart for the Palestinians. Prior to meeting this gentleman (who will remain nameless for security reasons), I had no frame of reference for anything Palestinian. An excellent book on the subject is *Blood Brothers* by Elias Chachour (Grand Rapids, Mich.: Baker Book House, 1984).
3. See Romans 12:4-8.
4. See James 1:17.
5. See Deuteronomy 26:19, Jeremiah 33:9, Esther 8:16.
6. Thomas A. Cahill, *The Gifts of the Jews* (New York: Doubleday, 1996), n.p.
7. See Genesis 12.
8. Cahill points out that prior to the Jews, the poetry and stories of other cultures did not have a beginning, middle and end. They might begin in the middle and end in the middle, with no sense of closure or conclusion, sort of like a child who forgets the punch line when telling a joke.
9. Gary Thomas, "The Return of the Jewish Church," *Christianity Today* (September 7, 1998), p. 63.
10. Romans 9:4,5.
11. The U.S. Center for World Mission publishes a monthly missions magazine

called *Mission Frontiers*. To subscribe, contact USCWM, 1605 Elizabeth St., Pasadena, CA 91104.

12. Part of the Buckwalters's story is told in *Missions Now* (Summer 1998), p. 7. Mennonite Board of Missions, Box 370, Elkhart, IN 46515-0370.
13. Ibid.
14. Ibid.

CHAPTER EIGHT

Honoring Cities

_And seek the peace of the city where I have caused you
to be carried away captive, and pray to the LORD for it;
for in its peace you will have peace._
—Jeremiah 29:7, NKJV

I once saw a hand-scrawled sign posted on the door of a church:
"Women wearing lipstick, nylons, jewelry, high heels, perfume,
or short hair may not enter this house of worship." Immediately
I perceived this wasn't exactly a 'seeker-sensitive' church. I'm not
sure what they thought might happen if a transgressing woman
had gone inside. Would she infect the rest of the tiny congregation? Were there no male "sins"? The sign would be laughable
except for the painful reality it represents. We can bar the door
to the table of God by being known more for what we're against
than for what we're for. We are often known more for our
denouncing of sin than for our devotion to our Savior.

In some people's minds, Christians are identified more by
their stand on political issues than for standing with the broken
and hurting. Say the word "Christian" to the non-Christian, and
it might conjure up images of a well-organized, front-range mili-
tia movement.

Too often our attitude of moral superiority has misrepresented God to our culture—to our cities. But God is turning the stance of the Church from a posture of accusation to hands that heal. We are becoming known as a people who bless and honor our cities and neighborhoods, and we're making a practical difference in hurting lives. In city after city, neighborhood after neighborhood, even as you read these words, God is loving people through His Church.

God is accomplishing this in very practical ways. We are no longer saying to pre-Christians, "Come to church, join, become like us and meet God." Instead, we are saying, "Let us serve you. How can we pray for you?" We are meeting with mayors and civic leaders to ask forgiveness for our past lack of blessing toward our cities.

Pre-Christians in our neighborhoods are beginning to experience Christians who care for their living environment, as well as their souls. In city after city, people are seeing their needs met with the warm welcome of God, because Christians are beginning to be seen as humble servants. God is bending us low with a basin and towel, and city governments are left speechless at the transformation.

AND THEY'LL KNOW WE ARE CHRISTIANS...

WITH A BASIN AND TOWEL

South Coast Fellowship, a West Coast church dedicated to selfless service, each year honors public school teachers by making them a hot lunch on in-service days. On one particular in-service day in a local high school, I remember my son, who was at that time four years old, standing on a milk crate in the school cafeteria, washing dishes in a big chef's apron. My heart was thrilled that he was involved in honoring public school teachers at such an early age.

He'll grow up thinking this is normal, I thought to myself. South Coast makes no overt attempt at evangelization at these dinners. They just make a clear and compelling statement that honors the dedication of public school teachers in our community.

They serve others as well. On the Avenue (a poor section of Ventura, California), a hot tri-tip roast dinner, with all the trimmings, was served in partnership with an on-site congregation to over four hundred neighbors surrounding the church. The dinner not only filled a lot of stomachs, it was also a wonderful example of one church honoring another by joining together to demonstrate the generosity of God.

At Christmas time, several churches combine to wrap presents for mall customers, free of charge. They serve hot apple cider and cookies and offer stress-reducing smiles. For the elderly and trusting, packages are carried out to the car. Doors are held wide open while mall customers are quietly prayed for and blessed.

Many churches across America encourage their people to do acts of kindness throughout the week. Some put change in expired parking meters. Others mow lawns. Some have even washed cars while people were shopping. Many of those who do such anonymous service leave a small business card with a phone number on it that reads: "We did this favor because God loves you! If you have any prayer requests, call us."

There are no limits to the practical ways you can bless your neighborhood and town. The Moms in Touch in one city made jam for the teachers at an elementary school. One pastor I know buys quality leather Bibles for all the county supervisors and has their names imprinted on them.

When we extend kindness to our city, we are saying to that city, "You are valuable and cared for. God loves the fact that you exist! We are honored to bless you, because God thinks about you constantly!"

THROUGH PRAYER

As recently as 1994, Covina, California, was not a very safe place to live. It was the murder capital in the geographical region of twelve cities that make up the East San Gabriel Valley. That year there were ten murders committed in Covina. In addition, there were drug-related crimes, and graffiti abounded. The city council and community were greatly divided over what to do.

In 1995, the community recalled the entire five-member city council. Chaplain David Truax called on the pastors of Covina's churches to join in regular prayer for their city. There was good response, and the healing began immediately. The group met on the first Thursday of the month in the briefing room at the police department. The results? The murder rate dropped by 90 percent in 1995, and crime in general continues to fall in the community. Gang activity fell so quickly, after the monthly meetings began, that the police department temporarily disbanded their gang task force for lack of need. It has only recently been reactivated.

During this period, Chaplain Truax was approached by a city councilman and invited to deliver regular invocations at the city council meetings. The pastors joined him in offering this new service to the community. Christians in Covina are still contending for all that God has for their city. There are no quick fixes, but God is using willing pastors to provide a canopy of prayer protection over their town.

GOD LOVES PEOPLE

Someone once said that the Bible begins in a garden and ends in a city. God loves cities. The reason He loves cities so much is because so many people live in them, and He desires for people to live and thrive in an environment of mutual honor.

I have a dear friend who was driving through a depressed area and musing to herself how pretty it must have been before there were tacky little houses and oil wells all over it. She immediately felt the Lord's correction: "To Me, it's much more beautiful now." She felt God's meaning to be that it was beautiful now because there were people there.

> *Honor is not a scheme for quick conversions, nor*
> *a subtle ploy to alter the behavior of people.*
> *Honor comes with no strings attached, no response*
> *required. We honor because God is honor.*

Every morning, God looks with attentive love as your neighbors wake and prepare for their day. There is no moment when His heart is not engaged with the people in your city. It is important that we see our cities with His heart and with His eyes.

Many years ago, when I moved to Ventura, California, I thought of it simply as a Greyhound pit stop on the road to God's ultimate destiny for my life. But through the years of living there, I came to love the city. I came to know its leaders and people, and my heart was sad to leave when I moved.

LOVING OTHERS IN JESUS' NAME

When we seek to honor people in our cities (to consider them valuable and significant), we do not screen them to see if their lifestyle is biblical. We do not insist they pass an orthodox litmus test. We don't run them through FBI screens to see if they're worthy. We don't distance ourselves for fear of contamination. We allow Jesus to be who He is, through us, to a hurting world. And we leave the ramifications to Him.

One great example of this happened just this year, in a city close by. Sonrise Christian Fellowship in Simi, California, had a choice to make. They could fear what other churches thought about them—they could be afraid of ruining their reputation by seeming to condone sin—or they could allow the love of God to be expressed through them in an unorthodox setting. They wonderfully chose the latter. So, at a Gay Pride parade, they had a concession stand that offered free water, sun screen and prayer. Guess which church, in Simi, a gay or lesbian might attend to investigate the claims of Jesus Christ? A church that offered them practical love and prayer or a church that stood in their face, protesting the wickedness of their lifestyle?

LOVING OTHERS WITHOUT STRINGS

When we honor people, it doesn't always change them. Jesus, knowing full well of Judas' intent to betray Him, honored Judas by washing his feet. While the God we love is not willing that any should perish, we recognize that not all will respond to His winsome love. When we honor others, we are expressing the personality of Jesus. Honor is not a scheme for quick conversions nor a subtle ploy to alter the behavior of people. Honor comes with no strings attached, no response required. We love others for the joy of Him who is love. We honor because He is honor.

When I was young, my parents used to minister on Skid Row in Los Angeles. I still remember the pungent smells of the men, the decayed hope that permeated their worn lives. I remember, too, feeling like we held them hostage for a meal. The mission my folks served required that the men sit through a sermon before they got their meager tuna fish or baloney sandwiches. It was if we were saying to them, "We know you're hungry, so we'll bribe you to stay and listen to what we say."

Honoring the people in our cities is not honor if we extend it with an ulterior motive. Honor is not the latest, hottest gimmick for successful evangelism. We do not serve our cities in order to fill our churches. We are engaged in humble servanthood because we're committed to demonstrating the personality of Jesus. It is not our job to save souls; salvation belongs to God. It is our joy simply to demonstrate a living, potent Savior. We joyfully exhibit the love of a Redeemer who felt at home with sinners and prostitutes.

I was coming out of the grocery store one day and felt a visceral reaction as I read the popular bumper sticker, "Practice random acts of kindness and senseless acts of beauty." It sounded so appealing. In our dog-eat-dog world, where kindness is rare, a sentence like that is warm and enticing. But in the phrase lies deep and serious error. God is never random in His kindness. He is intentional in all that He does. He has never been and never will be senseless in His beauty. His breathtaking displays of kindness and beauty are full of holy ambition. His acts are driven by fervent love. He has fashioned His kindness to lead us to the splendor of His Son.

When the Church in a city joins God in doing intentional (not random) acts of kindness, it is not to improve our image. It is to point to His image. He is the Father who waits day after day for the returning prodigal.[1] He is the One who longs to be gracious and waits to have compassion.[2] He is the One who wept over Jerusalem and said how often He would have gathered them.[3] When we show the tangible welcome of Jesus to our city, we honor God by representing Him well.

THE STORY OF CAMARILLO, CALIFORNIA

Lynette Bridges was probably clueless about what she was starting when she handed her pastor a clipping from a Sunday paper magazine insert. The article in *Parade* magazine was about an upcoming Make A Difference Day. This event celebrates one day a year when people band together in their communities and use their gifts and abilities to bless and honor their cities. This idea has caught on and is gaining momentum all over America.

Lynette's pastor, Rev. Steve Ditmar, thought the event sounded good and handed the project to a pastor on staff, Marilyn Norda. With Marilyn in the picture, a whole tsunami of volunteerism rose to engulf the town.

Marilyn went to pastors in the city and presented the idea. "Let's do it!" they said. She then went to the civic leaders and asked what needed to be done. The city lost no time in replying. There were playgrounds that needed fixing, trees that needed to be trimmed, schools that needed painting, sidewalks that needed cement. The list was enormous. There was so much enthusiasm for Make A Difference Day that the churches in the city decided to open it up to the whole town. Anyone, regardless of religion (or absence of religion), was invited to make a difference on one particular day in the city of Camarillo.

Every possible agency and civic institution was called and asked, What are your needs? What is your wish list these days? If you had a bunch of volunteers at your command on October 28, what would you have them do? The questions were met with grateful surprise.

Seabees from a local military base got in on the act. Construction companies donated material and labor. Catholic Social Services recommended seniors who needed help around the house. Children in public schools were each encouraged to bring a can of food to restock the food pantries for the poor. The newspaper gave free and copious publicity to the event.

It just so happened that Make A Difference Day that year coincided with the birthday of the founder of Camarillo, so the city thought it a perfect marriage—a day of volunteerism capped off with a fiesta of celebration that night.

A computer expert caught the vision and organized the whole event on a computer. A telecommunications company donated high-tech equipment and state-of-the-art walkie talkies. The event was organized to such an extent that the final count of people participating, including children bringing canned goods, was close to ten thousand people.

I asked Marilyn Norda recently about the long-term results of the event. Make A Difference Day resulted in favor with the city officials and forged lasting friendships. Christians in Camarillo are considered to be people who bless their community.

Cities all across America are being inspired by God to honor their cities with selfless service and tangible love.

IDENTIFYING WITH OUR CITIES

Within our cities we must take the posture of the intercessor, identifying with the pain and woundedness of our communities and crying out for mercy, or else we stand with the dishonoring accuser issuing condemnation. There is no middle ground.

Today, God is filling His people's hearts with bold prayers and visible demonstrations of His honoring love. He is also convicting us of our attitudes of accusation regarding cities. For example, in our local area, Santa Barbara is a jewel of a town. Its geography and architecture are unsurpassed in beauty. With all its loveliness, it is definitely the gorgeous older sister of the towns close to it. Ventura, too, is beautiful, but it doesn't have the stately, dignified beauty of Santa Barbara. Ventura is like a middle child. Its sense of itself is definitely less defined than Santa Barbara. And Oxnard, the next town below Ventura, has always suffered from an inferiority complex. Its name and its marvelous mix of ethnicity have conspired to assign it the role of stepchild in the minds of people who have lived there for many years and do not appreciate the beauty of cultures other than their own. Yet, people who are recent to Oxnard find it a gorgeous place to live. There are long sprawling beaches, acres of verdant farm land, gorgeous old Craftsman-style homes.

Why do people from out of town find something so desirable in Oxnard, and people who have lived there a long time make jokes about it? There is an unspoken yet long-standing culture of accusation against the city, and almost all of us who have lived outside but near Oxnard have participated in it. It is a subtle, insidious prejudice against the entire city.

Not long ago I was praying with some friends for Oxnard, and I felt the Holy Spirit's gentle correction. You see, I was born in Oxnard but I was so ashamed of the fact that I always quickly said, "But you know, I never lived there." I suddenly realized that all my life I had subtly sided with the accuser of that town and not the Intercessor, the Lord Jesus, who loves Oxnard and gave Himself for her.

SAN JOSE, CALIFORNIA

When we truly understand God's love for a city, it will be easy to serve that city. Pastor John Isaacs, of South Bay Covenant Church in Campbell, California, has been a vision caster for an event called "Churches Serving the City." The first year, 25 churches participated. Last year, over 40 churches joined together to honor San Jose and the surrounding communities with a day of practical, selfless service. Several thousand Christians pulled weeds, removed graffiti, painted park benches and planted trees.

Pastor Isaacs has encouraged Christians to speak blessing on their cities, pray blessing and become a blessing. Where the history of Christians in the city was previously confrontational, city officials have warmed up to Christians who are willing to serve. The mayor has met with pastors for prayer on several occasions. Christians in San Jose and Santa Clara Counties are becoming an instrument of blessing instead of cursing to their cities.

THE TANGIBLE TENDERNESS OF JESUS

In Danville, Illinois, a bomb tore through an Assembly of God church while a service was in progress. The blast injured 33 people, many of them teenagers. Days later, another bomb went off in the neighborhood of the church. This time the bomb exploded in the home of a man wanted for questioning in the first blast, and it took the man's life. The neighbors were evacuated, as agents from the Bureau of Alcohol, Tobacco and Firearms scoured the area for clues.

With the permission of his board, the pastor of the church, Dennis Rogers, appropriated funds to help neighbors repair their windows after the first blast. When the second bomb went off, Rogers negotiated with the mayor, the chief of police and the ATF to go into the area as the people returned to their homes. Rogers had $50 bills in white envelopes and $20 bills stuffed into his pocket. He knocked on doors, saying that the $50 was a love gift from his congregation. Then he reached into his pocket and said, "You know, your wife probably doesn't feel like cooking dinner tonight," and then handed the person $20 to help with dinner.

First Assembly could have gazed at its own wounds after the first bombing and adopted a bunker mentality. They could have lashed out at society's violence and injustice, accusing the culture of intolerance toward Christians. Instead these people chose to identify with the pain and woundedness in their own neighborhood and demonstrated in a practical way the tenderness of God.

In Cedar Rapids, Iowa, the Church in the city prayed weekly in the mayor's office with him and other pastors and city officials. The churches covenanted with God, at city hall, that theirs would be a "city of refuge." That prayer resulted in over thirty months without a murder.

The International Church of Los Angeles, also known as The Dream Center, encourages members to adopt a block in the drug-ridden neighborhood surrounding them. People who are brimming with the love of God, mow lawns, pick up trash and bring food to needy families in their chosen block. Since The Dream Center has opened, crime has been reduced over 40 percent in its immediate neighborhood. I asked some of the leadership how they protected their generosity from being abused. "We leave the abusers to God," they said, smiling.

Do our words and actions clearly communicate to our cities the personality of Jesus? Are we known for being people of honor? Might there be a day coming when you say the word "Christian" in your city, and the first word that comes to mind is "love"? The kingdom of God is a kingdom of honor, and it answers a strong "Amen!"

City Builder,

While we look for a city whose maker and builder is You, we live in cities right now that don't look anything like what You are building. There are people in our cities who are lonely and hopeless, and they need Your touch. Touch them through me. Love them through me. Pray for them through me. Show me practical ways to honor my city and the people who live there. Give me Your heart for my city. Let me speak honoring words about it. Increase Your fame in my town. Amen.

SCRIPTURES FOR MEDITATION
Jeremiah 29:7; Ezekiel 48:35; Luke 13:34

QUESTIONS WORTH ASKING

- In what ways have churches in your city honored your city?
- Are there needs in your town or city that could be addressed by you and your friends? Are there needs that you could begin to pray about?
- Is there something popularly said about your town that could be accusing?
- Do you hold attitudes about your city that God might want to gently correct?
- What is right about your city? Take a few minutes right now and make a list of everything that comes to mind.

Notes
1. See Luke 15:20.
2. See Isaiah 30:18.
3. See Luke 19:41; Matthew 23:37.

CHAPTER NINE

Honor Between Men and Women

*Be kindly affectionate to one another with brotherly
love, in honor giving preference to one another.*
—Romans 12:10, *NKJV*

I just about gave up the day for lost. Someone had cracked a joke
about the sound one pastor makes when he eats, and each subse-
quent speaker added fuel to the fire. National Day of Prayer
certainly wasn't going to win any awards for substance this year.

On top of that, the high wind and the central water fountain
at the county government center were threatening to make
Presbyterians of us all. It looked as if the day was going to be
memorable for all the wrong reasons.

Finally, the main speaker was given the microphone and he
began to speak, trolling his words like the seasoned fisherman he
was. Unexpectedly, his words evoked a sea change. Lawyers, who
were coming out of the hall of justice to get their lunch, paused
and looked puzzled. Secretaries from the administration building
turned their heads. As I listened, I did what I always do when
something holy is happening: I momentarily stopped breathing.

John Dawson said, "I may not be the guy who hurt you, but I am no stranger to male appetites. For every woman here today who was considered a sexual plaything in high school and then dumped for someone else; for those of you whose gifts and talents have never been taken seriously by church leadership; for you women whose intelligence has been dismissed and passed over in business because you are female, I repent."

The audience joined me as I continued to hold my breath. Jurors on their lunch break were straining to hear the rest. Unwelcome tears stung my eyes. I was embarrassed to find resonance in these nonpatronizing words. I had experienced unusual favor with church leadership at large. Being a woman had actually been to my advantage in advocating pastoral unity and prayer. Yet, here I was, hearing acknowledgment for the first time of a painful daily reality. Being a woman means being summarily dismissed by men.

As John continued to speak, the bad jokes were quickly laid aside and forgotten. Like a skilled surgeon of the soul, he probed sensitive, malignant tissue. Like a seismologist pointing out a hidden fault line, he exposed the foundational rift in human relationship, the subterranean dynamic that had prevented us from ever fully realizing God's intent in making us male and female.

God drew near. In spite of the terrible beginning, He was redeeming the day. Many women present had never heard a man apologize. This was something unusual. This was something to consider. Did God really feel this way? Was John accurately articulating God's heart?

Next to our need for restored relationship with God, the most radical reconciliation issue before us is the restoration of relationship between men and women. And we all intuitively know it. Lest you abandon this book, thinking me a raving feminist, let me tell you another story.

Several years after that National Day of Prayer event, I was sitting next to a pastor friend at a leadership luncheon. He said to me, "Fawn, I just don't get all this reconciliation business. I think it's gone overboard. Some of my guys don't even want to go to Promise Keepers this year over it. I am not a racist. I just don't think there's a problem."

I slowly swallowed my food, then turned to him and said, "You know, I've never had an ill thought toward you. I've always loved you and respected your ministry. But on behalf of women who never submitted to your leadership; on behalf of women who have been critical of your ministry; on behalf of women who have thwarted God's purpose in your church with gossip; for the women who have made cruel jokes about men, I repent."

My friend looked at me and said, "Oh." We finished our lunch, and moments later he invited reconciliation-prayer leader John Dawson to come speak to his large congregation.

THE TRUTH ABOUT MEN AND WOMEN

Jesus said the truth would set us free, which indicates that a lack of truth keeps us in bondage. When we explore the issue of honor between men and women, we are required to be dead honest. We have to trust God to reveal to us the things we don't want to see.

We are often like the boy, Eustace Clarence Scrubb, in The Chronicles of Narnia. Eustace was an annoying self-centered prig if there ever was one. And as the story goes, he went off by himself in Narnia and was lured into a dragon's den. In this den were mountains of gold and jewels; Eustace's heart coveted the treasure. He soon fell asleep. When he awoke sometime later, he was quite thirsty. He went to a nearby pool and was surprised to see a dragon in the water. He tried to figure out how a dragon could be looking up at him. To his shock and horror he realized he was looking at himself. He had become a dragon! Aslan the Lion (the Christ figure in the Chronicles) comes to the be-drag-oned Eustace and delivers him by extending his claws and swiping them into Eustace's dragon flesh. Tearing off huge chunks at a time, Aslan uncovers the now meek and completely humbled Eustace.

We have hidden our dishonor toward the opposite gender behind the masks of tradition, humor, scriptural interpretation and culture.

The story is rich in allegory. We, like Eustace, have become hard and scaly and fire-breathing. We do not trust each other. We have embraced myths about each other. We have had personal experiences that have verified our worst doubts about one another. Until we get thirsty enough to come to the pool of God's Word, we never realize the degree to which we do not resemble what God intended. We need strong courage to face the devastating, debilitating effects of our sin toward one another. But like Aslan, God is taking away all the excess. He is clawing away at our dragon flesh. And we are becoming humble and renewed.

If you are a man, it takes great courage to ask God how many of your attitudes about women find their source in culture, tradition and pride. If you are a woman, you need courage to ask how many of your attitudes about men find their source in wounding. Cancer does not disappear because we choose to call it another name. Both men and women need to look at the issue of honor from God's perspective. We need to see the systemic nature of our sin in our relationships with one another in order to fully understand our desperate need for healing.

We have hidden our dishonor behind the masks of tradition, humor, scriptural interpretation and culture. And the dishonor is not simply a product of masculine pride. Women, as well as men, have engaged in its death-dealing rhetoric. If you need proof, simply watch any sitcom on television. Whole galaxies of humor orbit around dishonoring the opposite sex. "I Love Lucy" and "The Honeymooners" made television careers out of exploiting male-female stereotypes. Old black-and-white movies display attitudes about gender that would be considered abusive today. If we outlawed men-women jokes, many comedians would find themselves short on material. If we were to erase the comments from the pulpit on this subject, many pastors would lose what is always a sure laugh.

The Scripture is clear. God's intent is for men and woman to share as joint heirs, expressing together His grace and gifts to a wounded world. Satan's ambition is, of course, to prevent that from happening. And he assures that outcome through the powerful dynamic of dishonor. Do you think it's because Satan knows that if this primary relational rift was healed, men and women serving together in humility would strike his kingdom a significant blow? By fueling a virtual blitzkrieg of dishonor between men and women, Satan skillfully prevents his own kingdom of dishonor from dismantling.

AFFIRMING ONE ANOTHER'S GIFTS

Chances are, when you think of biblical heroes, the names Lappidoth and Shallum are not on the tip of your tongue. Yet these men played a significant role in the destiny of Israel. Lappidoth[1] was the husband of the judge and prophetess, Deborah. Shallum[2] was the husband of Huldah, the prophetess during Josiah's discovery of the Law. Obviously, it wasn't common in Jewish life to have a wife with a prominent role in the nation. Being the husband of an influential woman in that culture was, as it still is today, costly to the masculine ego. Lappidoth and Shallum must have been men confident enough of their own manhood to allow their wives the freedom to be what God had called them to be.

Just as it is true that behind every great man is a woman who encourages him, so it is that behind every great woman is a man who calls her into a spacious destiny. You can be assured that if Lappidoth or Shallum had any reservations about their wives' calling, that calling never would have been realized. Lappidoth and Shallum must have humbly recognized God's anointing and favor on their wives.

How many other prophets or prophetesses could have arisen from the encouragement and nurture of their spouses? Only God knows. None of us come into our full destiny by ourselves. Honor sees not only the present but the potential future, and promotes others based on it. When Moses called a meeting for the 70 elders, and a few guys were heard prophesying outside the meeting, people complained. Moses' response was, "Would to the Lord that all God's people were prophets."[3] Honor does not seek to restrain and exclude but to enlarge and expand possibilities.

The whole issue of gender reconciliation is this: In humility, are we willing as men and women to lay down our perceived right to supremacy, to see God exalted? Do we want to see the perpetual honor of heaven being brought to earth in our male-female relationships? Will we intentionally ask God to deal with our prejudices about one another?

CALLING ONE ANOTHER TO GOD'S PURPOSES

DEBORAH AND BARAK

The story of Deborah and Barak is particularly instructive to us in this regard.[4] The children of Israel had been sold by God into the hand of Jabin, king of Canaan. Jabin, for 20 wearying years, bitterly oppressed Israel. Canaan had high technology armaments, and Israel had a forgotten God. So Israel did what they usually did when they were in a tight spot because of sin, they re-remembered God and cried out to Him. He answered and delivered them through a culturally unlikely pair.

Deborah was a prophetess and judge of Israel. She held court under a palm tree on Mount Ephraim. She is best remembered for doing an amazing and astounding thing. She used her influence and favor to call a man into his destiny and, thereby, saved a nation. Who knows what heart stirrings Barak had experienced in his quiet times with God? Did he feel any particular sense of calling? Did he hear God's voice summoning him in the night? We don't know, but we do know that Deborah sent for him and said,

> Behold, the Lord, the God of Israel, has commanded, "Go and march to Mount Tabor, and take with you ten thousand men from the sons of Naphtali and from the sons of Zebulun. And I will draw out to you Sisera, the commander of Jabin's army, with his chariots and his many troops to the river Kishon; and I will give him into your hand" (Judg. 4:6,7).

Then Barak said to Deborah something that Moses had said to God, "If you will not go with me, I will not go" (v. 8). It wasn't that Barak thought Deborah would protect him from injury. I think Barak was saying: Just as you've called me into my destiny as a warrior, so I am linking my destiny to yours and calling you into your destiny as a strategic leader who hears from God. We are in this together. Our gifts are incomplete without each other. I am not going without you.

On the battlefield, Deborah again encourages Barak. "Arise! For this is the day in which the Lord has given Sisera into your hands; behold, the Lord has gone out before you" (v. 14). In this story you have a threefold cord not easily broken. Deborah, Barak and God put the enemy to the edge of the sword until not one man was left in the army. Then, just in case we missed the point, General Sisera gets a tent peg through his temple at the hand of a lowly housewife named Jael.

I believe this is the model of how God will bring deliverance in the future—through men and women responding in humility and obedience to God and calling each other into engagement in the purposes of God. How many enemies of the Lord go unchallenged because we are busy quibbling over gender roles and responsibilities? How many enemies of the Lord go scot-free, because we have confused our cultural traditions with God's?

After the battle, Deborah and Barak recount in a duet the battle and the greatness of God. And there is a curious phrase in that song: "The stars fought from heaven, from their courses they fought against Sisera" (Judg. 5:20). Could it be that when God sees men and women calling each other into authentic destiny, with a genuine need for each other, that heaven itself will engage in the outcome?

SETTING A PLACE AT THE TABLE

Honor never dines alone. It sets a place at the table for others. Honor, like love, does not seek its own. Deborah and Barak sang a duet, not a solo. The song is a narrative tribute to the holy leadership of a man and a woman doing God's bidding together. A whole nation experienced deliverance as a result of this divinely initiated and merged calling of Deborah and Barak.

Perhaps the Spirit of God is saying to today's Church, "I'm tired of solos! I want to hear victory songs that are a duet between men and women." When you sing a duet, you have to learn how your partner breathes and interprets a song. You have to blend your voices. You are not simply focused on the song itself but on the person singing with you. God is sensitizing men and women anew to each other, and we are beginning to sing a few harmonizing notes.

I recently met with about 60 reconciliation leaders from around the world. There was no agenda to the meeting; we came for the express purpose of seeking God. One-day the issue of gender seemed to be on God's heart. I listened to a brother from Australia weep as he felt God's grief for the way women have been demeaned by men. I heard another man from Japan confess to God that he just didn't know how to do what he felt God was requiring, but he wanted to learn. One brother from Nigeria spoke of the struggle he felt on the issue, having attended a seminary that was prominently anti-women. A brother from Canada confessed that he feared what other men would think of him because he couldn't keep his wife under control.

One woman said she felt that Satan had planted a mantra in men's minds that they couldn't trust women. And everyone listened. There were strong tears on all sides. The interesting thing about the evening was that nothing was really resolved. And that was as it should have been. We often abort the full dealing of God in wanting neat closure to every issue.

Gender reconciliation is an issue we need to work out together for quite some time. We need solid biblical scholarship void of cultural prejudice. We are beginning to look at the issue through God's eyes, and we will need His wisdom and patience to not run over each other roughshod, even with truth. We need to give each other time to unlearn habitual patterns of dishonor toward one another. We need to extend grace, even as we challenge presuppositions.

DESIRING GOD'S FULLNESS FOR ONE ANOTHER

The prophetess Deborah's heart was for "the princes of Israel." I believe God is placing within women today a passion and desire to see men enjoy all that God desires for them. Honor desires God's fullness for all that God loves.

For many years, women in Lydia and Aglow, and other groups, have prayed earnestly for men to come into their full inheritance. I believe the Holy Spirit is making that happen today in many arenas—for example, the Promise Keepers phenomenon.

In the same way, male leaders today are acknowledging as never before God's gifts and callings in women. If God is the giver of every good and perfect gift, it stands to reason that if God gives a woman a gift of leadership, He expects that gift to be exercised. The issue is not one of gender. God is the Lord of the Harvest, and He places within people His gifts as He chooses. Honor simply recognizes what God has already done. One of the foundational dynamics of honor is that it does not seek to limit and restrict but to expand and include.

Those who understand the power of honor understand that we can never fully enjoy God's holy ambition for His people apart from each other. We were made in His image, both male and female. We were made to reign together. God will never be fully understood or enjoyed without the giftedness of both men and women expressing together His breathtaking character. Imagine the world's response to seeing Christian men and women out-honoring each other and preferring each other in love!

Male leaders around the world are freshly realizing the power of intercession. While intercession, like any of God's gifts, was never intended to be restricted to a female role (Jesus is the Great Intercessor), many intercessors are, at this writing, women. While avoiding the faddish dynamics of wanting an intercessor to simply make your ministry successful, many male leaders are seeing the value of listening carefully to intercessors. This new dynamic of leaders paired with intercessors is a small entry point for expanded Deborah-Barak relationships. Please do not hear me saying new dynamic *male* leaders paired with *female* intercessors. While for the most part that is the present reality, God, as the Lord of the Harvest, can appoint anyone He chooses to leadership or intercession. So we need to be aware that we can use spiritual dynamics to simply enlarge our own kingdoms. We must learn not to use one another.

General William Booth and his wife, Catherine, founders of the Salvation Army, labored powerfully together in England during the late nineteenth century. They saw God bring profound change to a blighted culture as they honored each other's call and gave wing to each other's gifts. From the beginning, the Salvation Army made a place for men and women to serve together to see God's purposes performed. I believe God is again going to raise up dynamic collaborations that will be powerful, compelling and culture changing.

INTENTIONAL HONOR

I remember talking with a white pastor who told me that racial reconciliation was not a problem in his church because he had one black deacon. He didn't understand what all the fuss was about. That man was allowed to attend and even was allowed a role in the church. To the pastor, the issue of prejudice was completely overblown.

I remember thinking, *Does he hear what he's saying? A man is allowed to attend, allowed to serve?* It reminded me of my own culpability in being unusually patient with someone who is terribly slow. My sin is that I'm aware that I'm being patient, and

I'm silently congratulating myself on being so godly. That very thought and attitude accuse me.

Gender reconciliation, like racial reconciliation, requires intentional engagement. A pastor does not have a racially mixed congregation because he says, "Oh, I'd be happy to have an African-American on staff if one ever came along that I thought was qualified." Honor intentionally seeks people out to promote. Those who are serious about gender reconciliation will intentionally seek to honor and give place. The best thing about having a platform of influence is to give that platform to others. Honor is intentional. It doesn't wait for someone to happen along worth promoting; it seeks that person.

Our model, of course, is the Lord Jesus. He intentionally entrusted the Samaritan woman with His first recorded disclosure that He was the Son of God. He intentionally let Mary be the first to announce the Resurrection. He allowed Lydia to be the first European convert of Paul. These were not accidental occurrences. They were fully intentional revelations. Jesus fully intends that the third millenium Church, His Bride, be made up of men and women honoring each other and giving place to one another, in humility and meekness. I believe the zeal of the Lord will make it so.

Father,

You are the One who made us in Your image, male and female. You are the only One who can teach us how to welcome each other into our destiny in You. Remove all the man-made barriers we have constructed against each other. Give us Your heart for one another. Raise up Deborah and Barak relationships that will bring deliverance to the captives. We look to You to do what only You can do. Amen.

SCRIPTURES FOR MEDITATION
Genesis 1:27; Judges 4—5; Ephesians 2:14-16

QUESTIONS WORTH ASKING

· How many of your views about men or woman are based in tradition or culture?
· Who comes to mind when you think of a modern Deborah-Barak relationship?
· Could you be holding subtle attitudes of superiority about the opposite sex? Ask the Holy Spirit to show you.
· Do you think God is limited by gender in expressing Himself to this generation?

Notes
1. See Judges 4:4.
2. See 2 Kings 22:14.
3. See Numbers 11:29.
4. See Judges 4—5.

CHAPTER TEN

Honoring Difficult People

Therefore let us pursue the things which make for peace
and the things by which one may edify another.
—Romans 14:19, *NKJV*

Quite a few years ago I worked for a man who was so difficult he
was borderline impossible. No one in the entire company could
please him. He was an angry, bitter man who spat out disdain
like some men spit tobacco. All the employees in the company
sought to avoid him, but because he owned the company, there
was really no place to hide. Christians were repugnant to him.
Knowing that I was a Christian, he intentionally hired me for a
sparring partner.

One day I found myself facing him and doing a curious
thing. I honored him. I honored him by telling him some things
I'd observed about him. I said, "You know, I've figured out three
things about you. You're a teacher, you love knowledge and you
have little patience for people who don't." He gave me a startled
look. No one had ever noticed that about him before. But I
didn't make it up. All of it happened to be true, and he knew it.

God opened a small door to my boss's heart through that
simple conversation. The Holy Spirit only needs a small door of

entrance to a heart. My boss didn't change radically overnight, but he softened toward me. We ended up going out to lunch many times and had some good talks about Jesus, and he gave me fatherly advice when I chose to leave the company. Honor was the God-initiated door to my boss's beleaguered heart. Today I still pray for God's goodness in that man's life.

CLOSE TO HOME

For many, the difficult person in their lives is not an employer but a close relative. Relatives who are difficult are often the greatest challenge to honor. We have no options but to relate to them. Our name reminds us of them. We have very real fears that we may grow to be like them. And we can't live as if they don't exist. Holidays and special occasions, instead of being joyful celebrations, become dreaded obligations. Difficult relatives can take the joy out of Christmas and birthdays and other important rites of our journey. A difficult relative can challenge even the most godly.

You would think Jesus' life was difficult enough but, yes, He too had difficult relatives. When it came to Jesus, His brothers saw only question marks. They doubted His divinity and thought Him mad. They even gave Him counsel about how to position Himself politically at the Feast of Tabernacles, sadly missing the opportunity to be His staunchest encouragers. It's comforting to know that Jesus knows exactly how exasperating difficult relatives can be.

THE LAW OF SOWING AND REAPING

Although it can be particularly painful if your difficult relative is a parent, God commands us to honor both of them. He puts no conditions on this command. We are to honor our parents. Period.[1]

God designed an impersonal law into the universe: What we sow, we reap. He intended that law for blessing. But like fire, it can be either a blessing or a curse. If we fail to honor our parents, we will reap dishonor in our relationships. It's as sure a law as gravity.

Honoring difficult parents is often the most daunting challenge we will ever face. But God promises long life to those who extend honor to them.

When your parents dishonor you, finding ways to honor them can be particularly difficult. In the case of physical abuse or severe verbal abuse, you must remove yourself from the violence. Perhaps you were sexually abused by a parent, your defenseless childhood stolen by the greedy hand of lust. Even to the depth of that unspeakable horror, God can grace you to forgive. He can grace you to extend grace. Honoring your parents is not contingent on their worthiness or your emotional strength to carry it out. You can forgive and seek to honor your parents as fully as possible, even if it's simply in your thought life.

You can always bless and honor difficult parents in prayer, if for no other reason than that they gave you life. And with that life they gave you the opportunity of knowing God and enjoying Him forever. No matter how hard your life has been, how inadequate their parenting, your parents gave you the priceless gift of life. All of God's goodness is available to you, including the chance to have intimacy with Him forever, simply by virtue of the fact that you exist.

God often uses family members to refine our character and show us who we really are. The Bible is full of examples of this. David's brothers mocked him when he went out against Goliath.[2] Job's wife sarcastically said, "Curse God and die, Job," as she served him coffee.[3] Hosea's wife wouldn't exactly have qualified for an award on Mother's Day.[4] The Bible is clear that the very first family was a dysfunctional one, and that has been true for many families ever since. It's rare to find a family that doesn't contain at least one particularly difficult relationship.

Difficult people show us who we really
are by our reaction to them.

While I don't believe God intends for us to play Sherlock
Holmes through our spirits, looking for sin, it's important that we
allow the Holy Spirit to do a thorough inventory of our attitudes.
Are we harboring resentment against our parents or other relatives? Do we ridicule them in front of others, or do we extend
grace and mercy to them, even as God has extended it to us? If you
are dealing with a difficult parent or relative, take it to the Cross.
The same blood that provides cleansing for you avails for them.

OUR BEST FRIENDS

Like fingernails on a blackboard or a fork scraping a plate, some
people are a constant grating aggravation. Almost everything
they do and say provokes us. And if tribulation works patience,
they do a terrific job. It's possible that the most aggravating
person in your life right now may actually be your very best
friend, from heaven's perspective.

You may be thinking that you'd be a lot happier if that difficult
person wasn't in your life. The reality is that God has allowed that
difficult employer, leader, pastor, relative into your life to teach you
some important things. He or she may be your best mentor.

One thing God wants us to work on is our response to difficult people. As I write this, America has a leader who has been a
moral disappointment to those closest to him and to the country as a whole. I believe God has placed this leader in our lives, as
Christians, to test our response to him. Will we "not speak evil
of a ruler of [our] people,"⁵ as the Bible commands? Will we bless
and honor him? Will we desire his good? Will we refrain from
salacious gossip and refuse to listen? I believe this leader is a

blessing because he has given us the opportunity to see ourselves as we really are. Our own response report card at this point appears to have some room for improvement.

Difficult people show us who we really are by our reaction to them. Are we sullen to them and sweet with everyone else? Are we generally warm but serve them a cold shoulder? Do they grate on us because they're incapable of seeing our strengths? Do we wish they would simply go away?

I have long grieved over a difficult relationship in my life and my lack of love toward that person. Because I'm considered a very warm and caring individual, the difficult person in my life keeps me from thinking too highly of myself. I see my own inability to love this person, and I weep for more of God.

MAINTAINING
AUTHENTIC RELATIONSHIP

It is no surprise that the Bible is one long chronicle of difficult relationships. As John Dawson observes, all sin is a sin against relationship.[6] Adam and Eve began the cycle by dishonoring their covenant relationship with God. Cain severed Abel's existence by murder. Jacob scammed Esau out of his inheritance. The ink is barely dry on the first chapter of our history before the story is brimming with broken relationships. The trail snakes on and ends up at our front door. None of us is immune. If you are alive, you have a difficult relationship in your life. You may be in denial about it, but it is nonetheless true. All human tragedy, all human history, can be summed up in the reality of broken relationships.

David and Saul, Paul and John Mark, you and _____; the list is as old as the earth. The very thing God gave us as the ultimate joy—relationship—is the very thing that Satan seeks to destroy. And Satan uses the weapon of dishonor to destroy it. Think with me for a second. You like to be around people who recognize your value and worth. You are uncomfortable around people who don't. Almost all difficult relationships relate to the subject of honor or dishonor.

Observe how God deals with the broken, difficult relationships in His life. Israel, His beloved Jeshurun, His covenant people, spurn Him and run after other gods. She provokes Him with her idolatries. She sleeps with just about anyone and breaks her marriage vows. And yet God woos her still. He, like-Hosea, honors her with an invitation to intimacy. He refuses divorce. Israel will never be replaced in God's affections. All day long He stretches out His arms to His people. He refuses to let broken relationships dictate His commitments. God's response to difficult people in His life is the clearest indicator of what He is actually like.

Of course, we are not God. Sometimes all we can manage is a polite smile. Sometimes trust needs to be reestablished. Sometimes authentic relationship will prove impossible. We occasionally must face that we will never be close to some of the difficult people in our lives. But God invites us to bless them. And we can bless them. In fact, we are to bless them and not curse them. We may not mar them with our private words of disdain; we may not joke about their eccentricities. If honor is to be extended to difficult people, it will be a result of us choosing to respond in the opposite spirit. We need the empowering love of Christ to enable us to honor those who seem unworthy of honor.

HONORING THE SEEMINGLY DISHONORABLE

Can we honor people who are unworthy of honor? The answer is a blessed and emphatic yes. We never honor sin, but we can honor and celebrate God's intense love for the difficult people in our lives.

I knew a man named Gary, a daredevil rascal who cared little for God or man. He was 6'4" and weighed at least 270 pounds.

Gary knew how to pick, and win, fights. As the head of a motor-cycle gang, he decided for kicks one day to roar motorcycles around an evangelistic tent while a service was in progress. The bellow of a Harley at full throttle can rattle a house. So imagine these poor people in the tent, trying to worship God, with a whole gang of Harleys circling round and round, drawing up dust and offense.

In the midst of the roar, the evangelist inside the tent did a God-inspired thing. He decided to honor Gary, and he chose to honor him with prayer. He asked the congregation to specifical-ly pray for the salvation of the leader of the gang. Not long after-ward, Gary came to know Jesus, went to Bible School in Rhode Island, and became an evangelist. By the time I met him, he had a heart as big as a Harley. We ministered to Cree Indians togeth-er one summer in Canada. Gary often wept for the goodness of God in his life.

The Garys of the world prove that we never know the end of the story for difficult people. We could be looking at a Saul breathing out threats to the Church and never guess he's five minutes away from an encounter with God. We could be seeing a Moses beating up an Egyptian and not realize that his hair-trigger temper will eventually be tamed by God to such an extent that he could be called meek and the friend of God. We might be hearing a Peter deny Jesus and think him to be the epitome of disloyalty and then see him a few weeks later full of the Holy Spirit, giving one of the world's best sermons.

We have no idea what God has in store for a person. Chuck Colson, a good candidate for the Democrats' most difficult person award, encountered God and became one of the preemi-nent prophets to this generation.

Remember the atrocities committed by the Manson family who murdered actress Sharon Tate, among others? Susan

Atkins, a member of the Manson family, has been a radiant follower of Jesus for over 20 years.

The list of the redeemed is endless. We could quote story after story of impossible people who have been tamed and transformed by the awesome power of Jesus Christ. In each case, someone honored them enough to honor them with prayer and to believe God had a destiny for them.

WHEN HONOR DOESN'T SEEM TO HELP

People don't always end up transformed when we honor them. But that's not why we do it. Life is never tame or predictable. Some people, no matter how you treat them, just get worse. Take King Saul, for instance. He was your prototypical difficult person, if there ever was one. Fueled by jealousy, he flung javelins at people[7] and kept company with demons. A fairly strong case could be made that he had a split personality. Yet David understood the power of honor and continually honored Saul, even at the peril of his own life.

Once, when David was running from Saul's murderous wrath, Saul went into a cave to relieve himself. It was the same cave where David was hiding. He was so close to Saul that he snipped off part of Saul's clothing to later prove that he had only good intentions toward the king. Another time, David stole Saul's spear while he slept. Yet David would not bring about his own destiny prematurely. David knew that he was God's anointed to take over as king of Israel, but he refused to promote himself by dishonoring Saul. In fact, David felt so keenly on the subject that he killed two people who had killed his enemies. They came to David expecting a reward; they paid with their lives. David refused to touch God's anointed. He lived as honorably as he could in treating Saul's kingship as significant. David honored God's command not to speak evil of a ruler of his people.

Another time, when David was fleeing for his life, a man named Shimei ran along the river and threw stones and cursed him. David's man, Abishai, was ready to pierce Shimei through, but David would not allow it. David said that perhaps the Lord had told Shimei to curse him.[8]

David's life was filled with difficult people: his brothers; his wife, Michel; his son Absalom; Saul; Mephibosheth; Joab—each one qualified easily as a person who did not merit honor, but David sought to honor God by honoring the difficult people in his life.

LOOKING PAST THE DIFFICULTIES

In the story of Jacob and Esau,[9] we see the healing dynamic of honor in difficult relationships. Jacob connived Esau out of his birthright and then scammed him out of his rightful blessing as firstborn. Esau was roaring mad and threatened to kill Jacob after the death of their father, Isaac. So Jacob beat it out of town to live with his mother's kin. Through a series of years of being scammed himself by Laban (a premier example of the law of sowing and reaping), Jacob is blessed by God and manages to return to his homeland with great wealth.

There is one slight problem. Esau, the cheated brother, is leading the greeting party. Had Jacob and Esau met years earlier, Jacob would have had only one life to lose. Now there were multiple wives and numerous children and many sheep and cattle. It was enough to make Jacob take out a life-insurance policy. He does a wise thing: He prays. And he heaps honor on Esau. Jacob prepares lavish gifts of animals for Esau. He plans his gift in stages, hoping to pacify Esau's anger.

Esau turns down the gifts, and here we have one of the most redemptive stories in the Bible. Jacob and Esau fall on each other's necks and weep. Perhaps Jacob is weeping with sorrow for cheating Esau. Perhaps Esau is weeping for his intent to kill his brother. Maybe they were weeping because they missed each other all those years that Jacob was working for Laban. Perhaps they wept for the mercy and goodness of God.

Paul and Barnabas had a major disagreement over team member John Mark. Paul felt so strongly about John Mark's unsuitability for the upcoming missionary trip that he parted with Barnabas, his good friend, over the issue.[10] Barnabas, the son of encouragement, had seen Paul's potential in God and risked his reputation to endorse him. Now Barnabas was seeing the potential of John Mark, but Paul only saw John Mark's flaws. Years later, Paul sent for John Mark, saying that he needed him.[11] What occasioned such a change of heart in Paul? We can only speculate. Perhaps Paul grew away from his self-righteousness and recognized his own sin, and compassion grew in his heart for others.

Perhaps, like Paul, you discern areas in someone's life that the Holy Spirit has not yet revealed to them. Because the Holy Spirit is an encourager and doesn't want to overwhelm us, He often gradually shows us the depth of our own sin. We never fully know ourselves; we are known only to God.

I am thankful for the choice friends in my life who have seen my sin, my self-righteous religiousness, my arrogance, and have loved me in spite of my brokenness. My friends did not write me off and alienate themselves from me. They chose instead to trust the Holy Spirit to deal with the issues of my life. Honor calls us to look past even accurate discernment and allow love to cover a multitude of sins.[12]

FORGIVING ONE ANOTHER

Joseph didn't know when to keep his mouth shut around his brothers. As a young man, he fueled offense by spouting true prophecies to brothers who did not care for his success. (Never

tell people who don't care about your success what God's promises are to you.) For years the brothers fumed with jealousy and
then decided to silence Joseph once and for all. They ended up
selling him to some traders who took him to Egypt. Joseph was
falsely accused and served a prison sentence, but through the
intervention of God, he ended up as prime minister of Egypt.

Years later, Joseph's brothers went down to Egypt for food
and ended up standing right in front of him. They didn't recognize him. Joseph now had the perfect opportunity for revenge,
and I imagine he toyed with the idea for a while. He made the
brothers sweat and played tricks on them. I believe God was dealing with his heart the whole time. Finally, in a tear-jerking scene,
Joseph revealed himself to his brothers. He recognized that what
they meant for harm, God meant for good.[13]

The difficult person in your life right now might irritate you
out of your skin, and Satan may intend your demise through that
person. But God's intention is to promote you through him or
her. You can never overemphasize the power of forgiveness. It is
the foundation of all human relationships. Jesus spent His life,
providing the means for us to forgive one another. He said, "Freely
you have received, freely give."[14] We have been the recipients of rich
mercy. We can give that mercy freely to difficult people.

When we understand how deeply God loves people, even
difficult people, it helps us to view a difficult person differently.
We know that we can be difficult, too, and God's love does not
waver toward us. Therefore, we see that God has been at work in
their lives, loving and correcting them as they allow Him.

I began this chapter with a story about my challenging boss.
What I didn't tell you was that I learned that his son (who was
Jewish) had a vision of Jesus and had become a pastor. That son
was praying for his dad. When I met the son, he said to me, "I
believe you are God's answer to my prayers for my dad." God so

loves difficult people that he puts us in their lives to demonstrate His love and forgiveness. We won't always do it perfectly; some days we might do it horribly. But God is able to grace us with the ability to try. It's obvious that God loves difficult people because He made so many of them, and we're included in their number.

Jesus,

You are no stranger to difficult people. Teach me how to honor them. Teach me how to see their gifts and acknowledge their abilities. Show me how to forgive them. Thank You that Your grace extends to them, just as it does to me. You are rich in grace and mercy. Show me what it means that love covers a multitude of sins. I cannot love them in my own strength, but I trust You to empower me to honor them. Help me not to just politely tolerate the difficult people in my life. I want to know Your heart, Lord Jesus. Please make it so. Amen.

SCRIPTURES FOR MEDITATION
Proverbs 10:12; 16:6; Matthew 5:44

QUESTIONS WORTH ASKING

· Without betraying his or her identity, what are some of the traits of a difficult person in your life?
· Are there practical simple ways you can honor that person?
· Meditate on a story in the Bible that involved a difficult person. How can you apply the story to your life? Ask God to give you insight.
· In what ways are each of us difficult people? Does God love us less for it?

Notes
1. See Deuteronomy 5:16.
2. See 1 Samuel 17:28.
3. See Job 2:9.
4. See Hosea 3:1.
5. Acts 23:5.
6. A private conversation with John Dawson, author of *Healing America's Wounds* and founder of the International Reconciliation Coalition.
7. See 1 Samuel 18:11.
8. See 2 Samuel 16:10
9. See Genesis 25–33
10. See Acts 15:36-41
11. See 2 Timothy 4:11
12. See 1 Peter 4:8
13. See Genesis 37–45
14. Matthew 10:8

CHAPTER ELEVEN

Honoring Children

At that time the disciples came to Jesus, saying, "Who then is greatest in the kingdom of heaven?" Then Jesus called a little child to Him, set him in the midst of them, and said, "Assuredly, I say to you, unless you are converted and become as little children, you will by no means enter the kingdom of heaven."
—Matthew 18:1-3, *NKJV*

John was in the sixth grade when his teacher, Mrs. McQueen, made an observation that would change his life. Instead of ridiculing his sometimes disruptive behavior, she praised his talent. "You have an uncanny ability to communicate with people and to make them laugh," she told him. God's call, and Mrs. McQueen's comments, helped to steer John Huffman into a successful pastorate where, today, thousands laugh at his ability to apply biblical truth to everyday situations.

Mrs. McQueen could have allowed herself to be irritated by John's comedic outbursts. His behavior in class definitely made her job more complicated. Instead she chose to see the underlying gift of the hyperkinetic class clown. By honoring John, she opened a door that showed him a glimpse of God's future for his life.

INVITING CHILDREN
TO A SPACIOUS DESTINY

Inside every child is a gift waiting to be unwrapped. Much like a fire opal, its exterior might be dull and unattractive, looking like anything but God-given treasure. A bossy child might have an unrefined gift of leadership. A shy child might be gifted with compassion. The gift possibilities are infinite and staggering.

Any adult, parent, friend or teacher can identify a child's gift and encourage him or her to unwrap it. It doesn't require prophetic insight; you don't have to have any special talent. All you need is a willingness to listen and observe. We honor children when we listen to them and observe them with careful eyes.

It's tragic to think of the untold numbers of children who could grow into adulthood with their gifts unopened and continue that way to the grave. Author and Bible teacher Dr. Miles Munroe says that the most expensive real estate in the world is the graveyard. How many unwritten symphonies lie in graveyards? How many scientific discoveries remain undiscovered? How many unwritten books? How many inventions? How many medical breakthroughs?[1] How much greatness lies buried beneath the soil for want of simple encouragement?

I know a highly gifted man who didn't do well in school because he couldn't see the blackboard. He didn't get glasses until the ninth grade. The glasses broke not long after, and he couldn't afford a second pair until he went into the military. What if someone had seen my friend's gifts and had given him glasses? What if he had been encouraged early on to explore his gifts? Our world is often deprived of greatness because we're too busy to encourage and nurture the gifts God has placed in children.

When we honor children, inviting them into a spacious destiny, we share in the reward of what they eventually become. Mrs. McQueen never pastored a church, but in God's eyes she played an important part in the success of South Coast Fellowship. A simple comment helped to shape John Huffman's future.

No one holds all the keys to him- or herself. People cannot fully unlock themselves by themselves. Honor functions much like a key that opens doors into a larger place, and each of us holds keys for one another. When I honor a child by acknowledging the child's giftedness, I open a door of hope. I give that child something to cling to when all of life seems to conspire against his or her dreams.

Some children's gifts come disguised. Betty Alverez Ham, the director of City Impact in Ventura County[2], went to various principals of public high schools and said: "Give me your most at-risk kids, for a leadership class; if you don't see a change in six months, you'll never hear from me again." Today, City Impact is in 43 public schools in our county and has more requests than staff to accommodate them.

Betty knew that the children who cause the most problems are quite possibly the strongest leaders. And she knew that potential leaders need strong instruction and good modeling to keep their giftedness from becoming destructive. While others have lamented the increase of gangs in our community, Betty and City Impact have been out with keys of honor, unlocking teenagers into a spacious destiny.

THE GIFT OF FUTURE SIGHT

While most people look at the present, others—Mrs. McQueen and Betty Alverez Ham—see the future. That gift of future sight is often what God uses to touch a child and catch his or her attention about destiny.

God saw the future of a little runty shepherd boy when his dad and brothers didn't even consider him worth including in the family picture. God told Samuel to go to Jesse's house to anoint the next king of Israel. Eliab, one of Jesse's sons, must have been an impressive guy, because as soon as Samuel saw him he thought, *Ah! This is the one.* But God said, "Do not consider his appearance or his height....Man looks at the outward appearance, but the Lord looks at the heart."[3]

Imagine the tension of the moment if you were one of Jesse's sons, standing in line with your heart thumping, asking yourself, *Will I be God's choice for king?* Seven of Jesse's sons passed before Samuel with no confirmation from the Lord, who was waiting for the one everyone else consistently overlooked.

"Is this all of your children?" Samuel asked Jesse. And Jesse replied, "Well, there's the youngest out tending the sheep." Samuel said to go fetch him; they weren't going to sit down until he came. So David walks in the door and walks out the anointed leader of Israel. When everyone else saw a shepherd, God, through Samuel, saw a king.

When everyone else saw a heartless gang banger, David Wilkerson, the founder of Teen Challenge, saw a future Christian leader and author in Nicky Cruz.[4]

The Early Church saw a young man named Saul (later called Paul) cheering the martyrdom of Stephen[5]; God saw the future writer of two-thirds of the New Testament. Paul's nephew could have been considered a nosey little snoop, but God saw a young man who would save Paul's life.[6]

People may have viewed Samuel in the temple as just another kid, but God saw a future judge and prophet.[7]

Simeon had the gift of future sight. He had been promised

by God that he would not see death until his eyes had seen the Christ. When everyone else saw just one more baby in the temple, Simeon picked the child up and prophesied, "My eyes have seen your salvation, which you have prepared in the sight of all people."[8]

Anna the prophetess saw perfectly with 84-year-old eyes as she took one look at the baby Jesus and saw the Lord's anointed. She spent the rest of her days talking about Him to all who hoped for the redemption of Israel.[9]

TAKING CHILDREN SERIOUSLY

Perhaps you are a Simeon or Anna, and you look at children with discerning eyes. If so, may your tribe increase. In our throwaway culture, it's easy to dismiss and overlook what God prizes. With technological advances decreasing our emotional capacity to cope, children can be a royal nuisance. They want our attention at the most inopportune times. They are loud when we crave quiet. They ask a steady stream of questions. They have no sense of timing. They leave a steady trail of themselves everywhere they go. Children are not convenient. Yet they are exquisite unopened gifts, simply waiting for a word to open them like flowers before the sun.

Children are often easy to dismiss because many of us adults are nearsighted, utilitarian in our outlook and frightfully occupied with the present. The disciples were just like us. They had a lot on their minds. There were a lot of important things happening around them. Jesus was becoming well known for His miracles, and His power could open some important doors. Being self-appointed guardians of Jesus' schedule, the disciples began to screen the people who could get to Him.

They didn't even think twice about children. Of what possible use could children be? They were a huge distraction from the important things at hand. If Jesus met with everyone who wanted to touch Him, He'd never do anything else. Children, of course, in the disciples' minds, were out of the question. After all, there was a kingdom to establish, prophecies to fulfill. But Jesus turned the disciples' thinking upside down. He took a little child in His arms and said, "Truly I say to you, unless you are converted and become like children, you shall not enter the kingdom of heaven."[10] And just in case we missed the point, Jesus welcomed the children and said, "Permit the children to come to Me; do not hinder them; for the kingdom of God belongs to such as these."[11]

The Spirit of Jesus in a child is every bit as powerful as the Spirit of Jesus in an adult.

Sometimes the Church, like the disciples, keeps children from getting to Jesus. It's easy to mark time, tell stories, sing songs and play games. But we can inspire them to discover their natural and spiritual gifts. We can challenge them to use those gifts in their communities. We can treat them as full-fledged members of the Body of Christ.[12] The Spirit of Jesus in a child is every bit as powerful as the Spirit of Jesus in an adult. Children are called, just as we are called, to wholeheartedly pursue God. What God is saying to the Church at large, He is also saying to children. Is God underscoring a season of prayer? Children can pray awesome prayers for other countries. Is the Holy Spirit highlighting a new passion to see the glory of Jesus cover the earth as the waters cover the sea? Children can catch a vision for something like the 10/40 Window.[13] Is the Holy Spirit under-scoring a season of fasting? I know children who fast television or chocolate. There is nothing that God is saying to the Church at large in the third millennium that He is not also saying to children.[14] Truth has no age restrictions.

Jesus was about His Father's business when He was twelve years old. Twelve-year-olds can experience God. And twelve-year-olds have much to teach us. Recently, in a Central American country, a pastor's conference was held and two young teenage boys attended. They were told this conference was specifically for pastors. It turned out that both boys were leaders in their churches.[15]

In Nicaragua, three twelve-year-old boys, who recently attended a child-care group run by the Assemblies of God in Managua, now regularly preach in revival meetings in Christian churches. One of the children already has his own weekly radio program. "We believe in the power of God to save," says the boy. "There are people in our country who need salvation. God gives us the courage to preach, so we do."[16]

At a recent conference, the Queen of Tonga called on Christian women leaders from Fiji, Australia, New Zealand, the Solomon Islands, Vanuatu, Papua New Guinea, Samoa and Tonga to present the message of Christ to every member of their family by the year 2000. The eighty delegates knelt before a large cross with their nations' flags while children prayed for them and their countries. Queen Mata'hao carried her nation's flag and knelt at the cross for prayer.[17]

We are beginning to recognize the inherent potency of a child's life with God. Most mornings, my son, Joel, and I cuddle and have informal talks about what God is like. As an eight-year-old, he's made some pretty startling observations. While some of his theology may be immature, it is clear that my son knows and enjoys God. At two and a half he came home one day from Vacation Bible School, put his hands on his hips and announced, "Today I gave my life to God." Joey and I take Joel's walk with God very seriously.

One morning, when Joel was about four or five, he walked into our bedroom and said, "I dreamed they caught a mackerel that was as big as the house. Well, actually it was as big as this bedroom." He then looked around and said, "Well, it was actually as big as your bed. They had to use a crane to haul it out of the water."

We were still trying to wipe the sleep from our eyes. My husband said to Joel, "Sure, sweetheart, that was an interesting dream."

A few days later a friend said, "Did you hear about that three-thousand-pound mackerel they caught in the China Sea? They had to use a forklift to haul the fish, it was so big!" I believe God gave this dream to Joel to show him that he could hear from God.

In the book of Joel, God promises that He will pour out His spirit on all flesh and that sons and daughters will prophesy, and young men will see visions.[18] We need to encourage our children to expect God to honor His Word. And we need to take children seriously when God does. History is full of evidence that children can know and love God passionately. They can be generous givers, their hands can bring healing, their eyes can see revelation and their prayers can undo ancient spiritual strongholds. God is not restrained by age in accomplishing His purposes. God can quite wonderfully express Himself through a child. Yet, sadly, if you follow the money trail in many churches, you will find children to be a low, or often nonexistent, priority.

D. L. Moody took children seriously. He was once asked how many converts he had in a particular meeting. He answered, "Two and a half."

The inquirer said, "You mean two adults and one child?"

"No," Moody replied. "I mean two children and one adult. The two children have their entire lives before them. The adult is half-spent."[19]

SEEING CHILDREN
THROUGH GOD'S EYES

We honor children by seeing them through God's eyes. John Maxwell[20] was in a class of elementary school boys when his teacher asked him and a few other guys to stay after class. "I pray for you boys every Saturday night," the teacher said, "and last night God told me you three boys would be going into the ministry." The teacher got down on his knees as he said, "I wanted to be the first to lay hands on you and ordain you into the ministry."

John Maxwell's teacher could have despaired at his students' perpetual lack of attention. He could have considered himself simply a lowly Sunday School teacher. But he took his job seriously. And he took his boys seriously. Most important, he took them regularly in prayer to God. He put himself in a position to bless God's desires for them.

I was a 12-year-old, waiting to talk to my hero, Audrey Mieir, when she parted the crowd surrounding her and embraced me and proclaimed to the people around her, "This child is going to be a writer someday." For over 20 years she kept in touch with me through letters, always scrawling a few sentences of encouragement. After Joey and I married, she invited us to lunch many times, sharing the secrets of her 50-plus years of amazing ministry. I never left an encounter with her without finding encouragement that I had a destiny and that God had great plans for my life.

Audrey had a lot of important, gifted people in her life. But she was not too busy to take notice of a scrawny 12-year-old with long hair and big dreams. Audrey's comments about me becoming a writer helped to keep hope alive when reason would have said to give up. She is one of the people responsible for this book.

What people think about us helps to mold who we become. Those who plant seeds of promise in a child's heart often create a destiny. We can partner with God in welcoming children into God's purpose for their lives. We can prophetically plant in the moist soil of a child's heart a future that God will nourish and cause to grow.

John Trebonius, the instructor of Martin Luther, always taught his class of boys with his head uncovered (a mark of honor). "Who can tell," he said, "what may arise from these boys? There may be among them those who will become learned doctors, sage legislators, nay, princes of the empire." Of course there was one student in his class, "one lone monk who shook the world."[21]

I have often walked by young men on the street who could easily pass for gang bangers. As I look them in the eye, with prophetic imagination I ask, *Which one of these guys are You going to turn into a pastor? Which of these young men, Lord, will end up giving his life for Your glory? What are Your magnificent plans for these guys?* The interesting thing is that without a word spoken, people can sense when you're looking at them through God's eyes. It's hard to be scared when you're looking in the face of a future pastor.

I once taught incarcerated teenagers. Many of my students had committed murder and other serious crimes. While the prevailing wisdom was to teach them to balance a checkbook and wear a condom, I had high expectations of what they could learn. I would bring them good literature that explored what it meant to be human. I would ask them to search the inner lands of their minds and hearts. I was aware that God could turn any one of them on a dime, capture their hearts and transform them. I knew that God had expectations for them that transcended their present reality.

BLESSING CHILDREN

God created the world using words. He said "Let there be light!" and light found joy and burst into being. He told the waters to be separated from the earth, and waves gushed to the edge of their boundary. God spoke worlds into existence. We, too, create a child's world by what we say. Our words shape and chisel; they bring hope or shame; they welcome or prevent a child from a spacious destiny.

As children, we sang the familiar lie, "Sticks and stones may break my bones, but names will never hurt me." We sang it almost like a mantra, trying to shield ourselves as the pain seeped into our spirits and colored our world. The truth was and still is that names hurt worse than sticks and stones. Children who have been victims of verbal abuse wear their black and blue marks on the inside where no one can see. Internal bleeding is harder to spot than external bleeding. Often, internal wounds don't show up for many years; and when they surface they are incredibly difficult to heal. A few short years of being called "stupid" or "ugly" can take a lifetime to erase.

Recently, in a wrestling match with my son, I made the mistake of calling him "goofy." He stormed out of the room as he said, "You may call me son, or call me beloved, but you may not call me goofy." Several hours passed, and he had talked very little with me before I realized I had wounded him. I apologized, knowing that what I had considered a term of endearment had carried, for him, the sting of reproach.

The Bible says that by your words you will be justified and by your words you will be condemned.[22] It is also true that by our words others are honored, and by our words others are condemned. With our mouths we can curse or bless children. We shape their opinions about God, themselves and their future with our words.

When we speak blessing over children, we release God's power in their lives. It is not only in the names we call them that we pronounce blessing, but it is also in the words we pronounce over them about what they might become.

PRAYING FOR CHILDREN

I still remember the warmth of her hand on my shoulder. I was on my knees in a prayer room after an evening missionary service. She was a missionary to Brazil, named Edie Adams, and she tenderly put her arm around me and prayed. She didn't pray a short perfunctory prayer either. She prayed a long considered prayer about my future. While I've long forgotten the words, at age 42 I still remember her touch and the fact that she prayed for me. You can give no greater gift to a child.

I began this chapter with the story of John Huffman. John had one other lady in his life besides Mrs. McQueen who would have an impact on him. She was a neighbor who was in a wheelchair and lived across the street. She thought John was an incorrigible hellion, but she prayed for him. Even though she had little faith in a good outcome, she prayed. And God, who rarely insists on perfect prayer, heard her cry.

Our prayers need not be limited to our own children. You can pray for children anywhere, at any time. You can pray in a checkout line when you hear a parent talk abusively to his or her child. Any time you see a school bus or pass by a playground, ripe prayer opportunities present themselves. And the prayer doesn't need to be long or profound. It can be as simple as "Jesus, you are worthy of being the talk of this playground. Please make it so." Often, I pass a child and silently ask the Lord that all His dreams for that child will come true.

Each of us has within us a desire to leave some indication that we once lived in this world. Gangs leave graffiti. Absalom, King

David's son, built a large tower. I heard a story one time about a man who offered millions to Princeton University to change its name from Princeton to his. Princeton refused, and the man was so bitter that he gave strict instructions that when he died, his body not be buried facing in the direction of that university.

When you honor children by praying for them, you leave an indelible mark that extends past your own lifetime. Audrey Mieir has been in heaven for several years, but her prayers and love for me as a child still live within me and before the throne. You can begin today to do something that will powerfully affect the course of history. You can pray for children. You can leave an eternal mark on future generations by your prayers today.

Charles Spurgeon has been quoted as saying that if you want to write something eternal, don't write it on granite where the weather of the centuries could erode the script. Don't write it on parchment where fire or age could destroy it. Write it on the heart of a child.

HONOR THROUGH TOUCH

Authors Gary Smalley and John Trent observe that, in the Bible, when children were blessed by their elders, touch was always involved.[23] In Mark 9:37, it is recorded that Jesus took a little child in His arms and said, "Whoever receives one child like this in My name receives Me." Jesus touched people.

Touch is one of the most extraordinary gifts you can give to someone. Medical studies have repeatedly shown the therapeutic power in touch. Endorphins are released with human touch. In a sex-preoccupied, litigious culture, touch has become suspect. While carefulness is always the dictate of wisdom, we honor and bless children by touching them. Our touch says, "You matter to me. I am not too busy for you. I am not too important to touch you." Touch can often communicate more than words.

I believe that this generation, what George Barna calls the "Mosaic Generation"—children born between the years of 1984 and 2002[24]—have a special call and destiny. God is going to raise them up to be a generation who seek Him.[25] They are going to have an unprecedented anointing to display God's power. We have a particular stewardship for this generation. We are privileged to bless and honor them. As we call children into a spacious destiny, we are engaged with God in forming lives beyond our own.

Jesus, Lover of little children,
    Give me Your eyes to see the children that surround me. Give me Your keys that will unlock their future. Touch them through my hands. Let me enjoy the honor of encouraging them. May they look back when they are old and remember Your love for them through my words. I am available, Lord, teach me. Give me the skill to love as You love, to see as You see. Make me a lover of children, like You. Make it so, Lord Jesus. Amen.

SCRIPTURES FOR MEDITATION
Matthew 18:3; Mark 10:14; Luke 2:25-32

QUESTIONS WORTH ASKING

· As a child, what adult recognized your gifts?
· What does the idea of encouraging children toward a spacious destiny mean to you?
· What biblical children were encouraged by adults?
· In your community, how are children honored?
· Take a few moments and ask God, "Is there anything You would have me do to honor children within my sphere of influence?

Notes

1. I am indebted to Dr. Miles Munroe for this concept of cemeteries being the richest real estate in the world.

2. Throughout this book there are many instances of events and people in Ventura County, California. I use them because this is where I live and these are the people I know. It would be a mistake to conclude that our county is experiencing all that God intends for it. We are very grateful for what God has done here, but we're very aware of how much remains for Him to change in us and our communities.

3. 1 Samuel 16:7, *NIV*, and John 7:24.

4. David Wilkerson, an inexperienced young preacher, began to reach out to several gangs in New York in the 1950s. One of the young men he tenaciously loved was Nicky Cruz. At that time, Nicky was the last person anyone would ever expect to have a future and a hope. His story is told in the book *Run, Baby, Run* (Logos Associates, 1988).

5. Acts 7:58.

6. See Acts 23:16.

7. See 1 Samuel 3:1-21.

8. See Luke 2:25-32, *NIV*.

9. See Luke 2:36-38.

10. Matthew 18:3.

11. Mark 10:14.

12. For an excellent resource on this, I recommend the book *When Children Pray* by Cheri Fuller (Portland, Oreg.: Multnomah, 1998).

13. The 10/40 Window is comprised of the 62+ countries that lie between the latitudes of 10 and 40, often referred to as the least evangelized real estate on the planet. For more information on the 10/40 Window, contact The Sentinel Group at 19109 36th Ave. West #206, Lynnwood, WA 98036 or call (425) 672-2989.

14. With the one exception, perhaps, of getting out of debt.

15. *Friday Fax*, September 13, 1998.

16. *Friday Fax*, September 24, 1998, reporting a story in *Religion Today*, 15 September 1998 by Byron Klaus of the Assemblies of God.

17. The Oceanic Women Renewed in Christ conference sponsored by the Lausanne Evangelism Committee, August 18-24, 1998.

18. See Joel 2:28.

19. An illustration heard in childhood, attributed to D. L. Moody.

20. Dr. John Maxwell is a popular author-speaker and is the director of INJOY Ministries, (800) 333-6506.

21. Paul L. Tan, *Encyclopedia of 7,700 Illustrations* (Dallas: Bible Communications, Inc., 1979, o.o.p.).

22. See Matthew 12:37.

23. Gary Smalley and John Trent, *The Blessing* (New York: Pocket Books, 1990).

24. George Barna, *The Second Coming of the Church* (Nashville: Word, a div. of Thomas Nelson, 1998).

25. See Psalm 24:6.

CHAPTER TWELVE

Honoring Old Age

*How far you go in life depends on your being tender
with the young, patient with the old, sympathetic with
the striving, tolerant with the weak and the strong,
because someday in life you will have been all of these.*
—George Washington Carver

It was a solemn moment, something none of us could have orchestrated. We had been asked to come and pray for a company's top management. Most of the executives were talented young men who had steered the company into profitable waters. Those gathered included the current young president as well as the former president, a handsome gray-haired man full of quiet dignity and wisdom.

While we were praying, a young man came over and got on his knees before the former president and began to ask his forgiveness. "On behalf of myself and any in this company who are young and have not honored you, I ask your forgiveness. For all the places we have taken the past for granted, for anywhere we have presumed our success was our own doing and not built on the sacrifices of the past, I ask you to forgive us."

I held my breath for the beauty and appropriateness of the young man's words. It was a priceless moment. Here was youth bowing low before experience, and articulating honor.

What makes this story so unusual is that it's so rare. As a culture, we worship youth, beauty and success. The elderly rarely come across our radar screens. We're often too busy to remember who they are and what they love. We have little time for anything that won't advance us and our own agendas. We have mentally discarded the elderly, warehousing them where we can. The few times we do honor them, we do it with our fingers tapping the table and our eyes on the clock.

Dishonoring the elderly has damaged us more than we know. Our children have perhaps paid the highest price. They have not received the blessing God intended to be handed down from generation to generation. Instead of being blessed and instructed by their grandparents, children have been parented by television. In many instances, their minds have been shaped by values and attitudes unfriendly to the ways of God.

WE REALLY DO
NEED EACH OTHER

Our highly mobile society has left us freighted with loneliness and isolation. Mother Teresa, in observing America, said that she felt loneliness was the leprosy of our day.[1] Our self-imposed exile from one another has resulted in perpetual inexperience.

How many marriages could we have saved had we asked those older than us to mentor us? How many bad business decisions have we entered into without good advice? How many children feel rootless and disconnected because they have no personal sense of their own history? How many consequences of sin have we had to pay for want of wisdom? We reinvent the wheel because we're too arrogant to inquire of experience or feel that we need any information from the past. We have no felt need for the elderly. In essence, we have said to them, just as we've said to conquered cultures, "You have nothing to give us; we have everything to give you."

God has blessed me with several older women in my life who have taken me under their wing and prayed over my present and future. When I was considering getting my master's degree, and my son was still a baby, one of these women said to me, "Don't you dare even think about it until Joel is at least seven! You can never get those years back!"

I heard the voice of God in her instruction, and I don't regret watching my darling son grow. I've been there for the unexpected questions you can't predict. I've heard his humorous observations about life. Loving him, and being present to love him, has been one of the joys of my life. I could have had a doctorate by now, but what I have instead is a heart full of splendid memories that are irreplaceable. I have those memories because I have a transgenerational friend in my life who wisely counseled me, and I listened.

I recently had breakfast with the same friend. I told her how sad I was that our churches have become homogenous camps of youth or the elderly but rarely a mix of both. I shared that I felt a billion people were going to give their hearts to God in the coming decade, but who would mentor them? Who would disciple them? I told her we had sent a message to the elderly that we didn't need them, they weren't desirable to us. Instead of challenging them to invest their wisdom and counsel in the next generation, we have encouraged them to go off to the J. Paul Getty Museum and have smiled politely at their concerns.

My friend replied that her generation also had sinned. They had not been flexible; they had not been willing to sacrifice their routines and tastes to see my generation come to God. They had been absent without leave from the purposes of God. We sat silently for a few minutes and realized how desperately we needed God and one another.

MUTUAL BLESSING

Consider the honor that Paul and Timothy showed one another. Timothy had a godly heritage. His mother, Eunice, and his grandmother Lois both loved and cherished the Word of God.[2] Timothy teethed on Scripture. It was all second nature to him. But because Timothy's father was Greek, and most likely an unbeliever, Timothy had a need for a father in the faith. He needed an older godly man in his life to call him into his destiny. I know countless young men like Timothy. I often see anointed, gifted young leaders, and my heart cries out for them the marvelous gift of a spiritual father.

Paul and Timothy were a strength to each other. We see Paul imprisoned in cold jails, comforting himself with the thought of Timothy, his son in the faith. Timothy—a young, inexperienced pastor—availed himself of Paul's extensive insight and revelation into the beauty and splendor of Jesus. Paul warmed himself at the fires of Timothy's future; Timothy warmed himself at the fire of Paul's passion for God.

Jack Hayford, when Church on the Way was growing beyond all projections, requested that two fathers in the faith join him on staff—Dr. Vincent Bird and Rev. Maurice Tolle. Pastor Jack wished to honor their years of service to God's kingdom as well as acknowledge his own indebtedness to the blessing they had been to him. Their prayer, wisdom, counsel and years of experience were a comfort to Pastor Jack, and he was a blessing to them. Their partnership wonderfully shows the divine reciprocity of honor.[3]

Several years ago, I was in Augusta, Georgia, at the funeral of Dr. Sam Sasser, who was a father in the faith to me. Many people spoke at his funeral, and they said many kind things about Sam. But it seemed as if their words would never have reached our ears if it hadn't been for the sound system. Then Judson Cornwall,[4] a father in the faith to hundreds of young pastors, got up. His words flew like arrows into our souls. He opened his mouth and God's perspective immediately came into focus. It was one of those moments when you realize the weightiness of experience.

God has designed age to provoke us to godly jealousy. We should look at those who have gone before us and covet what they have known and experienced in God.

Judson had spent a lifetime listening to God. His words were weighty because he had a long history with God. There is no substitute for it. You could be Mr. Mega-Anointed City, and if you're young there are certain things you can't bring to the table. God has designed age to provoke us to godly jealousy. We should look at those who have gone before us and covet what they have known and experienced in God.

As a young child I read over and over *Hudson Taylor's Spiritual Secret*, and my heart burned to know God as Hudson knew God. I remember 20 years ago, hearing Dr. J. Sidlow Baxter pray. I could not for the life of me keep my eyes shut. Here was an elderly man radiant with love for Jesus. Here was a man who knew God. Had I been a young man, I would have apprenticed myself to him in a heartbeat.

PRESENT HONOR, FUTURE BLESSING

RUTH AND NAOMI

In the story of Ruth and Naomi, we see how the honor that a younger woman shows to an older woman becomes the door to inheritance and blessing that has perpetuity. This blessing has affected all generations ever since.

No soap opera could top Naomi's story.[5] First there is a famine in Israel, so she moves with her husband to a foreign land. Those who have lived somewhere other than their native culture can attest to just how lonely that can be. Recently my husband and I built a house in another city, just twenty minutes from where we had lived for twenty years. Twenty minutes away can feel like a different state when your roots are fifty feet deep in your hometown.

Not only was Naomi separated from her people, but shortly thereafter she was also separated from her husband by his death. Ten years later her two married sons die. Now all she has left is two daughters-in-law, an empty heart and the threat of starvation. Where was all the goodness God had promised His people? Where was all the joy? Naomi's life was an insurance underwriter's nightmare.

Naomi hears that the Lord has visited His people with food, so she decides to return to her hometown of Bethlehem. She changes her name to "bitterness" and begins to pack up her belongings. Her two daughters-in-law get together and decide to go back with her. She's obviously touched, but she encourages them to stay in their native land. Orpha kisses her mother-in-law good-bye, but Ruth pours out her heart in a passionate pledge of undying loyalty. She tells her mother-in-law that she will go wherever Naomi goes—Naomi's people will be her people, and

Naomi's God will be her God.[6] It is one of the most tender sentences about a covenant relationship you will ever read. Here is a young woman pledging her future to an older woman who is only related to her by marriage.

Ten years before, Naomi had gone out from her homeland full. Now she was coming back empty. She was close to penniless as she reentered Bethlehem. Her husband was dead. Her sons were dead. All she had going for her was a stubbornly committed daughter-in-law who cared for her. Naomi could have ended her days a bitter old woman, but she ends up by bouncing a healthy grandson on her knee. This drooling darling will become the grandfather of King David. All because Ruth understood the power of honor.

All of Bethlehem is amazed at Ruth's loyalty. She is the talk of the town. She goes out to glean barley grain after the reapers have finished, and she catches major landholder Boaz's eye. Ruth obviously could have set her heart on someone younger, someone more handsome. But she responded to Boaz's kindness. Under the cloak of darkness she comes and sleeps at his feet, as was the custom of the day. She asks him to spread his mantle over her, indicating that should he want to, he could marry her. Boaz is overjoyed at this unexpected honor.

Here we catch a glimpse of God's intent for mutual honor in all our relationships. First, Ruth honors Naomi by pledging never to desert her. Naomi honors Ruth by talking highly of her to the women of Bethlehem. Boaz honors Ruth by becoming her kinsman-redeemer. Finally, God honors Boaz and Ruth with a son, Obed, the grandfather of King David. God's ultimate honor of Ruth is that He includes her, even though she is a foreigner, in the family tree of His beloved Son. God never leaves honor unrepaid.

Ruth's story richly illustrates the spiritual potency of honor. Back in Moab, Ruth has no idea she will end up famous. She does not honor Naomi because she has a contract for a starring role. She honors Naomi from the heart, and God responds from His heart by honoring her in return.

We never know what God will bring out of our willingness to honor the elderly. We, like Ruth, are clueless to the spiritual ramifications of our actions. One day my elderly dad called and said that some people in his town had come and cleaned his house and yard. Afterward they had prayed with him. Could their honoring of him with a gift of service have opened his heart to the love of God? It's possible my dad may now be in heaven because some people honored his age and served him. Someday, I will know.

We rarely know what our honor will reap in our lifetime. Ruth didn't know that Obed would become the grandfather of King David. She had no clue that she would be the great (times fourteen generations) grandmother of the baby Jesus. She didn't know that millions of children in Sunday School would learn her story. She had no idea that in millions of marriage ceremonies her pledge of loyalty would be quoted.

The story of Ruth also teaches us that our own future is connected to our present honoring of those older than ourselves. God makes this clear in the commandment that ties our long life to honoring our parents. We shorten our life through dishonor. We destroy our own future by our disdain.

MARY AND ELIZABETH

Mary, the mother of Jesus, and her cousin Elizabeth also experienced the mutual comfort of a multigenerational friendship. You can imagine being thirteen or fourteen and feeling the shock and stress of discovering that you were about to be a mother, without human intervention. Not just any mother, mind you. You were about to be the mother of the priceless Son of God.

One time my son asked me, "Mom, would you rather be the mother of me or the mother of Jesus?" I thought it over for a while and said, "Sweetheart, I'd rather be the mother of you. Being the mother of Jesus might be quite intimidating." Joel replied, "Yeah, but you'd never have to remind Jesus to clean His room!"

Shortly after the angel's dramatic announcement, Mary decides to visit Elizabeth, who is also with child by miraculous means. Although their miracles are different, they are both pregnant. We don't know what was in Mary's mind when she decided to visit Elizabeth. All we know is that she stayed for three months. Jack Hayford comments,

> It's not hard to imagine a multitude of ways the younger woman would have worked around the house, gone to the well for water, shopped at the market. Her cousin was quite aged and was advanced in the term of her pregnancy. So who can measure what Mary's diligence and loving service may have meant to her senior-in-years cousin in assuring the success of Elizabeth's pregnancy.[7]

Elizabeth faced the added complexity of a husband who is unable to talk for nine months. Perhaps that was a blessing, or perhaps it was one more challenge. Again, we don't know. We can easily surmise that Elizabeth needed someone to talk to. It's not every day you get pregnant the same day your American Association of Retired Persons card comes in the mail.

Because God designed all relationships to thrive in an environment of mutual honor, it is safe to assume that Mary profited as richly from her time with Elizabeth as Elizabeth profited from Mary's presence. While Mary may have been serving Elizabeth, God was most likely using Elizabeth to speak into Mary's heart wisdom and courage for the days ahead. The same

God who made us for relationship, gifted the two of them to experience a miracle together. God wants to overjoy us with miracles. He delights in intervening in our lives against all odds. At whatever point of impossibility, He can step in and change everything. Ask Sarah. Ask Elizabeth. Ask Mary. God is not confined.

MENTORS FOR THE YOUNG

As the Church in the third millennium begins to understand the power of honor, we will come to profit from the strength, perseverance and wisdom of those older than us.

Of course I realize that life is not like "The Waltons." While God's intent is for past generations to bless the future, and our future is tied to our blessing their present, sometimes it's not easy. Some parents and grandparents need God's touch before their influence can be a blessing to future generations.

I came to realize the depth of this while standing outside a board of education meeting. Quite a few Christians had come to protest the adoption of a sex education curriculum. I had gotten there late and so was standing in the parking lot when a teacher friend came up to me. She was visibly upset and said, "You Christians have no idea what we're contending with! You think everyone has parents who care about them. I have students whose parents encourage them to get pregnant, so they can draw more welfare money. When are you going to wake up and realize the world is not a two-parent caring family?!"

I felt convicted by her words. We, as Christians, tend to think that all families are wholesome and have their children's best interests at heart. But this is not always the case. Some environments are abusive and destructive. This situation makes honoring difficult and seemingly impossible. But God has not left us without options. We can always bless and honor difficult relatives with prayer. And you can always find little ways to remind them that you remember who they are and what they love.

The fact that some senior citizens are not in a position to be an example to the young increases our desperate need for seniors who are willing to mentor and love the younger generation. Children who do not have older people in their lives are bereft of a specific love that cannot be substituted. We ignore our need of this at our own peril. When we honor those who are older, we honor God. We make a statement that living life well is an art we need to learn from those who have come before.

Ancient of Days,
  Thank You that You will never stop loving me because I am too old. Your love endures, and nothing can separate me from it. Give me a heart to learn from those who are older. Let me understand Your plan for blessing. I want to honor You by honoring the elderly. Teach me how. Amen.

SCRIPTURES FOR MEDITATION
Psalm 71:18; Proverbs 16:31; 20:29; Isaiah 46:4

QUESTIONS WORTH ASKING

· How will honoring senior citizens positively affect the future?
· How would you describe someone in your life who provokes you to godly jealousy?
· How was Mary and Elizabeth's friendship mutually satisfying?
· In what ways might God call you to honor seniors?

Notes
1. Mother Teresa made this comment at a presidential prayer preakfast in Washington, D.C.
2. 2 Timothy 1:5. Lois is the first named grandmother in Scripture.
3. Jack Hayford, *The Mary Miracle* (Ventura, Calif.: Regal Books, 1994), p. 167.
4. Judson Cornwall is an author-teacher who has written over 15 books. One of my favorites is *Praying the Scriptures* (Lake Mary, Fla.: Creation House, 1990).
5. The book of Ruth is richly illustrative not only of a transgenerational relationship that God blessed but also of Jesus, our Kinsman-Redeemer.
6. See Ruth 1:16.
7. Hayford, *The Mary Miracle*, p. 169.

CHAPTER THIRTEEN

Honoring the Helpless

"He judged the cause of the poor and needy; then it was well. Was this not knowing Me?" says the LORD.
—Jeremiah 22:16, *NKJV*

Jasmine[1] never enjoyed the warm comfort of a mother's hand tenderly stroking her face. She never knew the pleasure of a parent who felt joy in her existence. She was born blind and facially disfigured; her mind did not work well.

During the critical formative years, Jasmine, along with her deaf and blind sister, were kept locked in a dark room. They were fed under the door like animals at the pound. In Jasmine's family, children with disabilities were barely kept alive. For five years she lived exiled from hope. For five years no one had the faintest idea that inside of Jasmine a wonderful gift waited to be opened.

Then one day something wonderful happened. Jasmine and her sister were placed in a home for disabled children. In this home, love was spoken and honor understood. It wasn't long before Jasmine discovered music. The director's wife patiently taught her to play the piano. Soon she surpassed her teacher.

Now she took lessons in the city. Seven of my Lydia friends and I sat speechless as Jasmine sat at an old upright and played classical music. She was even willing to play requests. I asked her to play my favorite composer, Debussy. We listened with wonder and moist eyes.

This home full of miracles is in a little town outside Bethlehem. I was filming Palestinian children for an upcoming prayer video. Someone had given me two first names and a hastily scrawled phone number on a little piece of paper. I called and was warmly invited to come right over. After a harrowing taxicab ride with a driver who carried his own weather system, we finally arrived in Edward and Hellene's home. We were graciously received and listened to astonishing stories about the children they loved and served.

Edward spoke to us in gentle, measured tones, describing miracles as if he were simply telling us the time. As he talked, he tenderly cradled a small child in his arms who could not move. Pain had hammered her delicate features, turning them into a slight frown. The child was much older than her size. She had stunning eyes. She also had a feeding tube sticking up from her face and seemed only capable of blinking. Her eyes occasionally searched Edward's face when he stopped talking. It was clear that she took comfort in his voice and the closeness of his chest. His stories about the children were astounding, and he spoke without self-consciousness and without the slightest taint of self-promotion.

One girl was autistic. He told us how she had been hungry to see her image and would show a slight response to a mirror or a piece of glass. She would climb up into Hellene's lap, not to receive the generous love of this gracious lady, but to see her reflection in Hellene's eyes. She would dart unexpectedly across the street while they were shopping, to stand before a store window. She did not look at the merchandise; she wanted to see her reflection.

But here she was now, a tall young woman of sixteen, from all observation healed of autism. She laughed with ease as she worked with the other children. I was amazed at the transformation. I had never heard of anyone healed of severe autism. At first I thought I may have misunderstood her story; maybe I had the wrong person. But no, this was the girl. She had been healed by love.

A seven-year-old boy caught my eye. Within seconds I had swept him up into my heart. Handsome, with a warm dreaminess, he'd been beaten by a family member and gone blind in one eye. Here he was now, soaking up love with an engaging, slightly crooked smile.

Elena, on the other hand, was a bomb in the process of detonation. She was incapable of a whisper and talked incessantly. All of nine, she'd never met a subject on which she didn't have an opinion. Her boisterous voice and endless energy exhausted me. But this was not always the case for this kinetic fireball. Elena was born with her insides outside of her body. Edward and Hellene had seen her through multiple surgeries abroad. She had become a daughter to them and lived noisily confident in their love.

I looked out over Bethlehem from the living-room window, marveling at the poetry of God. This was the city where love first made its entrance. This was the place where honor came, wearing flesh and bones. This was the city where a homeless baby shook the world. Two thousand years later, honor was still wearing flesh and bones in a tender middle-aged Norwegian couple empowered by the love of Jesus. When I asked Edward why he did what he did, he said, "The Muslims say to me, of what use to the world is that baby? It is deaf; it is blind; it cannot hear or read the words of the Koran. It will probably die before it reaches the age of five. Of what use is this baby?" And then Edward told me his answer: "I tell them, yes, this baby cannot see or hear, but she can feel. She can feel that I am holding her close to my chest. And when she dies and goes to heaven, she will meet Jesus, and she will know she has been loved and held by Jesus throughout her earthly life."

A REFLECTION
OF OURSELVES

To a discardable society, people like Edward and Hellene will never make sense. We value production. We are card-carrying members of the cult of beauty, youth and success. In this cult, deformed faces and limbs don't belong. In this cult, if you can't be beautiful, you can at least be productive. All the inconvenient babies, deformed children and old people end up aborted, warehoused and removed from our sight. We don't have time for the useless. We don't want to see them, lest it remind us of our own weakness and mortality. Yet, in looking at the deformed, we see ourselves. They mirror us. In them we see an external view of our own internal reality. The truth is, we too are deformed. Each of us, even the most stunning of bodies, have severe internal defects. We are born selfish, stingy and irritable, and we want things our way. We are, as C. S. Lewis observed about himself, "a zoo of lusts, a nursery of fears and a whole harem of fondled hatreds."[2]

Law and culture serve only as a thin veneer to keep us all from killing each other and exposing our true selves. A friend of mine was in Rwanda shortly after the genocide. I asked her what surprised her most. She said she had observed both in Rwanda and Bosnia how quickly ordinary people can turn into murderers.

Truncated versions of our original design, we hide our deformity behind business suits and semi-politeness.

THE BEAUTY OF GOD'S MERCY

This is the reality that honor addresses. We cannot, in and of ourselves, ever truly be loving, beautiful or useful. Stunted by sin, our functionality is never fully realized. We are, in fact, as helpless as the Palestinian babies and children Edward and Hellene spend their lives loving.

When we honor the helpless, we honor God. When we consider them to have value and significance, we affirm the divine mystery of God's love. God doesn't love us because we are useful or beautiful. He doesn't love us because we are capable of giving Him emotional satisfaction. He doesn't need or lack a thing. We cannot add or return value to Him. He is, in and of Himself, complete. We are not necessary to Him. The marvel of God's love is this: He loves us completely, in spite of our lame, crippled hearts.

God had no illusions in creating Adam and Eve. He knew before creation that man would choose to reject and rebel against Him. The Bible says that the Lamb was slain before the foundation of the world. God knew, and He paid the price of giving us choice. And yet, His love compelled Him to create anyway. Because God is a God who loves, He had His heart fully invested in us before any of us drew our first breath. Like a parent watching an ultrasound, God was aware of our potential deformity and uselessness. But because of His all-encompassing love, He chose to honor us by breathing into our nostrils His very own breath. He honored us by taking what was inside Him and putting it inside us.

My friends Derek and Renee Loux know this marvelous aspect of God's personality. Their son, Josiah, was born with

spina bifida. During one of the many times Josiah was hospital-
ized, Renee heard nurses in the corner muttering about the fact
that she should have had an abortion. She went over to them
and expressed her appreciation for their work and then said, "I
am fighting for my son's life, and I need you to know that I
would have had him, even if all he was had been a beating ear."

*By honoring the weak we become demonstrations
to each other of the expansive, unfading love of God,
who pledges to never leave us, to never forsake us.*

Josiah loved people richly in his own inimitable way.
Although he couldn't talk beyond a few words, he would reach
out and pat people's faces as if to say, "There, there, everything
is going to be just fine." Derek and Renee profoundly loved their
little son. Derek carried him like a proud papa everywhere he
went. Josiah lived and loved and left a trail of blessing for two
and a half years. When he died, he left Derek and Renee rich with
enlarged hearts. Because of Josiah's unconditional love, they
know God's love better. They now speak with compassionate
identification to parents of suffering children.

The Josiahs of the world teach us that honor is not something based on utility. We do not exist to be used by God but to
be loved by Him. He is not in need of skilled factory workers to
extend His kingdom. He does not need worker bees to spend
their lives serving and sustaining Him. He needs nothing. He is
not basing His love on our performance or productivity. He
loves us because He *is* love.

By honoring the weak we come to know the vastness of God's
personality. We become demonstrations to each other of the
expansive, unfading love of God, who pledges to never leave us, to

never forsake us. He is a God who honors His vows. He is not a man that He should lie. He is the God who said He will not break a bruised reed or snuff out a smoking flax. To all the broken and useless, God loves to show Himself strong and immense with love.

Considering people to have value and significance extends as well to those who are mentally frail. In honoring them, we underscore how each of us desperately needs the loving touch of God. I have an acquaintance who in no way commends herself to what I find enjoyable in a person. I intentionally have high-impact, low-maintenance friends. She is neither. She is mentally weak, naive, simplistic. When she calls, I consciously have to keep myself from brushing her off. I am always tempted to hide behind busyness and ignore her overtures of friendship. Yet I secretly know we are really not all that different from each other. Each of us is only a trace element away from mental illness. And so I choose to honor her by listening when she calls. As I listen, I try to imagine what God has in store for her in heaven. She will most likely be dazzling, and I will weep for the place of honor God gives her in His land.

HONOR NEVER DINES ALONE

David, the man after God's own heart, set a permanent place at the his table in order to honor someone who was weak. Mephibosheth,[3] Jonathan's son, was five years old when three terrible things happened to him all in one day. His grandfather Saul and his father Jonathan were killed in war. As if that wasn't enough tragedy, his nurse, on hearing the news, left in a flurry and dropped him. It must have been a significant fall because we are told that for the rest of his life Mephibosheth was lame.

Because of a prior covenant made to Jonathan, King David wanted to show the kindness of God to any relatives of Saul. David finds out that Jonathan's son, Mephibosheth, is still alive.

David generously gives him three things. He restores to him the land that his grandfather Saul had owned. He gives him servants to till the land. And David gives him a place of honor at his own table as one of his sons.[4]

Honor does not dismiss; it includes. Honor says, "Here; sit beside me. I've made a place for you."

JESUS IN ALL HIS DISGUISES

Mother Teresa understood this power of honoring the helpless. She made a life of picking up maggot-eaten bodies and caring for them tenderly until they died. It would be easy to romanticize how people responded to Mother Teresa's love. While some were grateful, many were too ill to respond at all, and some resisted. But for Mother Teresa, she was not seeing them. She was seeing past their faces and seeing "Jesus in His many distressing disguises."[5]

Showing the kindness of God by honoring the hurting, costs us. It is never convenient and it is rarely fulfilling. But sometimes astonishing things happen. Jean-Dominique Bauby was the editor in chief of *Elle* magazine. In 1995, he was left completely paralyzed by "locked-in syndrome," a stroke that severed the connection between his brain and body. He could not breathe on his own and he could not speak or eat. He could not move any part of his body except his left eyelid. His friends thought he was now a part of the produce market.

But with his left eyelid Jean-Dominique Bauby did an astounding thing. He wrote a book. His stenographer estimates he blinked in code over 200,000 times. His stenographer would start with saying the most common letters, like *E*, and Jean-Dominique would blink when the stenographer had the right one.

Jean-Dominique wrote a 130-page book called *The Diving Suit and the Butterfly*.[6] Part of his purpose in writing was to prove his intellect superior to a radish. Many so-called friends took one look at him and walked away in disgust. Imagine if Bauby had been completely dismissed by everyone. Someone honored this apparently useless man and discovered a vital, intelligent human being. Someone valued Bauby enough to pay attention. But what if he wasn't able to write a book with his left eyelid? What if he was for all intents and purposes brain dead, as well as body dead? What then? Do we only honor those who have the potential to respond in some meaningful way?

Jesus forever cinches any misunderstandings we might have about the power of honor. In a shocking passage in Matthew 25:31-46, Jesus commends the righteous for meeting Him when He was hungry, homeless, naked, sick and in prison. His hearers are incredulous. When did we ever see You like that, Jesus? And Jesus replied that when they did it to the least, they did it to Him.

Not everyone will turn out to be a piano player like Jasmine or an author like Jean-Dominique. We have no guarantees that honor will produce anything but pleasure to God. But considering people significant, listening to them valuing human life in all its expressions becomes a constant reminder that God will never leave us. He will not forsake us when we are no longer able to carry our fair share. When we are faithless He remains faithful still. We are never for one moment discarded by God. By honoring the useless we become a visual aid to ourselves of the magnificent love and faithfulness of God, an unswerving faithfulness that beckons us to know that nothing can separate us from His love.

THE POWER OF HONOR
IS THE POWER OF GOD

In an age when the gospel is regularly reduced to what we can get, it can be misleading to use the words "power" and "honor" in the same sentence. When we use the word "power," we associate it with position and external results. If you are powerful, people will give you things. If you are powerful, you can make things happen. But honor doesn't do the things we normally associate with power. Honor doesn't necessarily advance you or get more stuff for you. It isn't a magic talisman that, when applied, grants you luck or good fortune.

Many of us treat God like a refrigerator, going to Him and looking over His shelves, aimlessly wondering what we're in the mood for at the moment. God is not on a mission to make us comfortable or wealthy. We need to want God for God alone.

Often we will see a set of principles, say, for city reaching. We enact those principles to the letter and then are highly displeased when the results do not meet with our expectations. No virtue of God should ever be trivialized into simply another formula for success. God is not a formula. He especially is not an ingredient in a formula. He is Himself. He will be who He will be. And He will do what He will do. And He will not duplicate Himself.

The power of honor happens on a much deeper level than the material. When we honor the helpless, we demonstrate in practical terms the God who loves us in all our frailty and neediness. The power of honor lies in God Himself. We cannot honor anyone, including God, apart from Him. Otherwise, all our attempts at honoring others will be tainted by jealousy and self-interest.

And we are self-interested to the bone. We calculate how our relationships will advance us; we are nicer to people who hold more promise in promoting our agenda. I once stood on the balcony during a major Christian conference and watched as the speakers fawned over a Christian philanthropist. Would he have been given the best seat in the house if he had no money? Would he have been invited to sit on multiple organizational boards by simply the virtue of his wisdom and love for God, if he were only living from paycheck to paycheck? Probably not.

It is important to realize that we can never express the personality of God apart from God Himself. He is the Father of Lights, from whom every good gift comes. We cannot sustain any portion of goodness without Him. We are shipwrecked on the mercy and goodness of God when it comes to expressing genuine honor to the useless. Because of our own preoccupation with self-interest, it will never come naturally to us.

God fuels our ability to operate outside our own self-interest. Ask any wife who is serving the needs of an elderly, infirm husband, and she will tell you she cannot do it day in and day out apart from being sustained by God Himself. You may find yourself at this very moment caring for someone who gives very little in return. God will empower you to show honor, to value and to treat that person with significance. He gives Himself freely to those who acknowledge their neediness and inability. When we make a conscious choice to honor the infirm, we are inviting God's expansive love to enlarge our own hearts.

Father,

Thank You that You never break Your vows to us. You never discard us. You will not cast us away when we are no longer useful. Our hearts and future are secure in Your love. May we demonstrate the reality of Your unfading love to the weak, the infirm, to those whose minds and emotions do not work well. Make us a strong illustration of what You are like in Your attentive love. Amen.

SCRIPTURES FOR MEDITATION
Psalms 41:1-3; 82:3,4; Jeremiah 22:16

QUESTIONS WORTH ASKING

· Is it true that God did not make us to use us, but to love us? Why or why not?

· When we demonstrate love to the weak, what are we saying to ourselves?

· Can you think of a story in the Bible that illustrates this chapter?

· Do you know someone helpless that you could honor this week?

Notes
1. Not her real name.
2. C. S. Lewis, *The Inspirational Writing of C. S. Lewis, Surprised by Joy* (New York: Inspirational Press, 1986), p. 124.
3. 2 Samuel 4:4.
4. 2 Samuel 9.
5. Jaya Chaliha and Edward LeJory, *The Joy in Loving: A Guide to Daily Living with Mother Teresa* (New York: Penguin Books, 1996), p. 65.
6. Anne Swardson, "A Tale of Courage Told in a Blink of an Eye," *Washington Post,* March 11, 1997, p. A1.

CHAPTER FOURTEEN

Honor in Language

For then will I turn to the people a pure language, that
they may all call on the name of the LORD, to serve
him with one consent.
—Zephaniah 3:9, *KJV*

Professor Higgins only had a few months to win a wild, seemingly impossible, bet. In the stage play *My Fair Lady*, the professor wagers a significant sum that he can take a shrill flower-selling commoner off the streets of London and pass her off at an upcoming royal ball as a poised, aristocratic lady. He intends to do this amazing feat by simply changing how she talks. The professor surpasses his own enormous expectations. Not only does he turn Liza into the talk of the royal ball, but she is also mistaken for royalty herself. In the process of all this, Professor Higgins falls in love with her.

That is exactly what the Holy Spirit is bent on doing with us. He is already in love with us, but He wants to change the way we talk. God has big dreams for us (marriage to His Son, for one), and He is going to pull it off. The truth, though, is that we are in much worse shape than Liza. We are an unlikely bride. Like Liza, we are shrill and uncouth. We do not speak the gracious language of honor. For instance, take Christian radio. While there are many broadcasters who honor Jesus, it is a sad fact that many of our broadcasts are full of dishonor toward those with whom we disagree.

We are not yet ready for the marriage supper of the Lamb. We talk like the world talks. We've forgotten that words matter. In a culture loud with verbalized confusion, we've become deaf to the death rattle of our own language.

Author and priest Henri Nouwen tells of riding through Los Angeles and having the sensation he was driving through a huge dictionary. "Wherever I looked there were words trying to take my eyes from the road. They said, 'Use me, take me, love me, drink me, smell me, touch me, kiss me, sleep with me.' In such a world, who can maintain a respect for words?"[1]

We speak evil of our rulers.[2] Our language drips with offense and unforgiveness. We are bitter and hard. We spit out our words like a baseball pitcher spits chew.

If language is the litmus test of our souls, we are in dire need of a doctor. We force our words into tightly caged definitions that keep us from taking responsibility and acknowledging our sin. We did not sin, we were indiscreet or our behavior was inappropriate; we do not gossip, we are simply giving all the facts so people can pray intelligently; I wasn't a glutton last night, I ate "a little too much." Our speech is shot through with self-protection and accusation. We use language to hide our own sin and point out another's. We say things we don't mean and mean things we don't say. We jest and reveal our own paucity of spirit. Just this past week I walked away from several conversations where I felt I had betrayed a friend just by listening to someone else poke fun at him.

In ministry circles, confidential information that could shatter another person's future is often shared with ministry peers who have no pastoral need to know. Not long ago, I was scheduled to minister with someone fairly well known. Just before I left town, another minister friend said, "Oh, is so and so ministering again? I thought he had taken a sabbatical because he was still wrestling with _____."

Of course this comment colored my relationship with the individual, even though the person in question had submitted to leadership and removed himself from ministry for an extended time. The person had been broken and humbled by the tender hand of God and was walking softly before Him. His ministry was poignant, honest and powerful. But my heart had been tainted by confidential comments about him, and it took me several days to regain my equilibrium.

We have shed blood with our tongues and left a trail of crushed hearts in our wake. How many pastors leave the ministry over the continual criticism they have sustained? How many people are not in fellowship with God's people because of gossip and accusation? Our undisciplined tongues have driven more people away from God than we care to count. None of us are free of the blood guilt of an untamed tongue.

LEARNING A NEW LANGUAGE

The Holy Spirit is undeterred from accomplishing His task, despite our neediness. He is teaching us to speak pure words. We are learning a new language, a language of honor. We are being convicted as never before by what comes out of our mouths. God is raising His eyebrows at how we traffic in information about each other. He is creating holy hesitancies about how we use humor to ridicule. We are allowing that conviction to have its perfect work, and we are slowly, maybe even some days imperceptibly, being changed.

Pastors are making covenants to not speak ill of each other. Leaders are on their knees, weeping in repentance for our words against our brothers. Just the other day I was with a group of regional prayer leaders who wept together in repentance for our arrogant words against the Catholic Church. We are beginning, even if haltingly, to learn the language of honor.

Eugene Peterson makes the observation that all speech is answering speech.[3] We have been listening to words since our exit from the womb (some would say even earlier). Before we utter our very first word we have had millions of words spoken to us. We do not initiate speech, we respond to it. We talk because we have been talked to. The nuances of accent and brogue are imitated by us because we have absorbed them, often unconsciously. The melody of speech becomes our song by repetition.

My son, Joel, has an enormous vocabulary. One evening we were at a restaurant with a few friends and we were talking about the word "innuendo." We asked Joel if he knew what the word meant. "Yeah, of course. It's like 'double entendre,'" he said without batting an eye. Joel has a big vocabulary for an eight-year-old because he's around adults all the time who speak big words. He speaks because he has been spoken to.

In North America, our language reveals our location of origin. Someone from Canada pronounces the words "out" and "about" differently from an American. In New England you don't eat "corn," you eat "con." And who can resist the honey-dripping drawl of the Southern states? On a good day, I can identify someone from Minnesota in about three sentences. I have an English friend who pronounces words marvelously. When she says the word "extraordinary," it awakens eternity in my heart. How we speak betrays where we are from. Like Liza, in My Fair Lady, our upbringing or lack of it is immediately apparent in our speech.

The language of honor is the native tongue of the kingdom of God.

If that's true, I fear we've been living in front of our television sets more than in the presence of the Lord. Our speech is more informed by radio and television than it is by the Word of God. In the final analysis, there are really only two languages: the language of honor and the language of dishonor. The language of honor is the native tongue of the kingdom of God. But often the Bride goes slumming and speaks the street slang of hell.

As we immerse ourselves in the Word of God, we find the language of honor informing our prayers, creating right heart attitudes and providing a basis for relationship. The truest indicator of how one thinks may be how one speaks. James said that bitter and sweet water should not flow from the same stream.[4] Those who speak the language of honor, pray and love best.

THE LANGUAGE OF HONOR

To learn the language of honor, we must listen to its author, the Lord Jesus Christ. In Him we see honor spoken, spelled out, pronounced repeatedly and amplified. Hearing His words, listening to the tone in which He speaks, enables us to speak His heart into an aching, noisy world. To a culture blaring with the idiom of dishonor, we bring the gift of pure speech.

God, in describing His Son, calls Him the Word made flesh, dwelling with us. Flesh did not precede the Word, the Word preceded flesh. The Eternal One is the Word. Everything that we consider desirable and good is the description of the personality and character of Jesus Christ. The language of honor is true, right, pure, lovely and excellent. The language of honor flows out of the Word Himself. He not only teaches us how to speak, He *is* the Word. He *is* the language. Our speech is answering speech to the beauty of His person. Our speech is responding speech to the marvel of who He is. We are given the gift of language to express Him—His desires, His intentions, His way of relating.

When we speak words that are not true of Him, when we pervert words to slash and wound, we wound Him.

HONOR SPEAKS IN HUMILITY

We find the first primer on the language of honor in the book of John. "In the beginning was the Word, and the Word was with God, and the Word was God...and the Word dwelt among us, and we beheld his glory...full of grace and truth."[5]

God's passionate involvement with humanity shows stunning humility. God, the maker of heaven and earth, the creator of all worlds, chose to come live with us in the flesh. He who fills all heavens pitched His tent on our very own front lawn. Jesus reserved for Himself no executive privilege. He perspired from our weather, probably had childhood diseases, experienced indigestion and suffered indignities that we as flesh know all too well. We weren't prepared for what Ken Gire describes as "God cooing from the stable."[6]

"Who is like the Lord our God, who dwells on high, who humbles Himself to behold the things that are in the heavens and in the earth?"[7] God unrobed Himself of galaxies of honor and privilege to wear our tattered garb of humanity. Yet we've become dulled to the weight of the Incarnation. This extraordinary event has devolved into a sweet, sentimental story. Yet, Jesus' birth proves that the language of honor is spoken up close, in person, face-to-face.

It is honor that brought Jesus to Bethlehem. He who was not confined, humbled Himself on entrance, hemmed in by fragile lymph tissue. He became like us, vulnerable to the common cold and diarrhea. His humility has forever dignified us with His presence. Just as a piece of art is only worth what someone is willing to pay for it, Jesus paid the highest price possible to make a statement of our value to Him.

The language of honor is spoken in humility. "The fear of the Lord is the instruction of wisdom, and before honor is humility."[8] This tone of humility is instructive for those of us who have wrapped ourselves in self-righteous robes and stood at great protective distance from those with whom we disagree. The disagreements may have been social, political or doctrinal. They may be rooted in private disdain of race or gender. Often there is a sharp divide simply over methods, personalities and phrasing. We have justified our distance by sanctifying our perspective and have built entire empires demonizing others.

But honor comes up close. It is willing to talk. It does not withdraw. If we are to honor men because they are fashioned in God's image, then we can never distance ourselves from them. Honor does not allow us to indulge in the subtle haughtiness of spiritual pride. Jesus did not come to us at a distance, sterilized and hermetically sealed. He did not approach us with holy clinical reserve. He did not shout at us God's pronouncements. The whole drama of God's interaction with man is one long story of passionate up-close involvement. God is not afraid of contamination; He invites our touch.

MORE THAN MOVING LIPS

The language of honor is not just audible, it is visible. We see the language of honor spoken today in the host of nameless men and women who touch those who ache, who smell, who can no longer help themselves. One man, John Bills, a Youth With A Mission (YWAM) leader in Los Angeles, tirelessly and tenderly serves those dying of AIDS.

History is shot through with examples of those who understood the language of honor. One man was Father Damien. He spent sixteen years of his life, until he died, with the lepers of Molokai, Hawaii. The government, fearful that leprosy was contagious, tore mothers away from their children and fathers from their sons and moved them to an island from which it would be impossible to escape.

Father Damien chose to live with the lepers on their designated island. Missionary contemporaries of Damien felt that leprosy was God's judgment. They felt disdain and contempt for the native population. But Father Damien understood the humility that brings honor. He not only chose to live among them, but he also bandaged their wounds, laid the host wafer on their tongues and willingly placed anointing oil on their foreheads. Damien dined with his lepers, preferring to say "we lepers" rather than "my brethren."

Damien honored Hawaiian lepers with the gift of presence. He spoke the language of honor, eventually dying from leprosy himself. Honor draws close in humility and does not step back. It does not pay only lip service, it pays with its life.

Have we drawn close to our culture in humility? Has the world seen us on our knees in repentance or have we strutted about making pronouncements of judgment on other people's sins? Have we been afraid of contamination?

A FOUNTAIN OF LIFE

Have you ever noticed that you like to be around people who say nice things about you, and you feel wearied by people who don't? Last year a few friends took me out for my birthday and wrote in cards what I meant to them. The words nourished my soul. I did not pass the cards around because they were too precious, too private. Could what they say really be true? Perhaps my friends were following God's example of calling those things that were not as though they were.[9] I found their words a fountain of life.

In Ezekiel 47:9, the river of God makes everything it touches grow. The language of honor has the same effect. Everywhere it speaks, things grow. It is a creative language. We have all known people with green thumbs. My mom can take the most desolate of plants and make it grow. Often she has rescued a bedraggled plant that no one would pay five cents for. By her touch she has nurtured it to a thing of beauty.

I have a friend who has a green tongue. He can make just about anyone thrive. He does this Miracle-Gro wonder with words. The language of honor has the power to create.

Dishonor, on the other hand, is a language of death. When it talks, things wither. The book of Proverbs says that with his mouth, the wicked man destroys his neighbor.[10] I have listened to mothers publicly berate their children in grocery check-out lines, calling them horrid names. And I have wanted to run over and cover that child's ears. The harm inflicted in a moment of rash speech can last a lifetime. Our words are never neutral. We are either speaking life or pronouncing death.

A TRUTH TELLER

I have to admit that Jesus seemingly said some pretty dishonoring things. He called a woman a dog. He told the Pharisees they were white graves and viperous snakes. He called Herod an old fox. He upbraided His mother for asking Him to do a favor. Just a casual glance at the record would indicate that Jesus let loose some rather scorching statements. Did Jesus always speak the language of honor? If honor is the language of the kingdom of God, then what are we to make of all the unpleasant things Jesus said?[11]

Of course we weren't there to hear the tone in His voice. We weren't there to see if there was a glimmer of invitation in His eyes when He told the woman with a demon-possessed daughter that He was not sent to dogs but to the lost sheep of Israel. We don't know if, during one of His severe responses to the religious hierarchy, there was an undertow of invitation, welcoming them to wake up to their duplicity and follow Him. Was there a sob in His voice when He overturned the moneychangers' tables in the Temple? Was there honor in simply being willing to converse with hardened hearts bent on His demise?

I think we miss the awe and marvel that Jesus was willing to talk to the Pharisees at all. Most of us would have slammed the receiver down when they called during dinner. But Jesus was just like His Father. Throughout the entire history of the Jews, God cajoles. He pleads. He uses metaphor. He writes poetry. He makes His prophets into billboards. He constantly and continuously communicates to those with missing ears. G. Campbell Morgan makes this observation about the prophet Jeremiah:

> The fact that having spoken, and been disobeyed, God should continue to speak; the fact that He should persistently speak, when there was no immediate response; the fact that He should continue to speak when He knew there would be no response; and, that under such circumstances, and at such a time, He should speak...these are among the most interesting and remarkable things in our old testament scriptures.[12]

That Jesus even engaged in dialogue with the religious hierarchy was a sign of His unwavering persistent hope in the possibility of their transformation. We only have to look at Paul to see Jesus' hope justified. Yet, I think Peter gives us the best clue to the hard sayings of Jesus. Peter, the disciple we can identify with most, finally had a good morning. For once he'd opened his mouth and something profound had come out. Jesus had asked the disciples about His identity. Peter answered with uncalculated certainty, "You are the Christ, the Son of the Living God."[13] Jesus commended Peter and changed his name from pebble to stone, and said He would build His church on the foundation of that revelation. It was indeed a very good day.

Shortly thereafter, Peter's joy evaporated. When Jesus spoke of His impending death, Peter simply said, "Far be it from you, Lord!" And Jesus turned and said, "Get thee behind me, Satan, you are an offense to me for you savor not the things that be of God, but those that be of men."[14] Satan? That's worse than being called an old fox or a viperous snake. I can just hear Peter's grandchildren say, as he tells them the story, "Oh, come on, Grandpa, Jesus didn't really call you Satan, did He?"

Didn't Jesus passionately love Peter? Why did He speak so severely to one of His closest friends? Where was the language of honor then? This exchange with Peter is a clue to all the other harsh things Jesus said. The language of honor is a language of truth. It does not fudge or pretend; it does not court favor in order to promote itself.

In contrast, we have Absalom at the city gates, feigning concern, kissing hands, judging people's disputes (you can imagine the judgment being weighted in favor of the presenter). Absalom massaged frail egos, using them all the while as steps to the throne. The language of honor is a language of truth. Because Jesus is the Truth, He cannot lie.

Jesus loved Peter too much to allow Satan any room in him. When Jesus called Peter Satan, it is the diagnosis of a doctor who is scrubbing His hands for an emergency operation. "Peter, your thoughts are malignant. We must operate at once." When Jesus called the Pharisees viperous snakes, it was intended to provoke them into looking in the mirror and seeing the reality themselves. God longed for them to be His holy, beloved sons. Jesus was always ready to cure the diagnosis if the sick one acknowledged the truth.

Remember the lady who approached Jesus for the healing of her daughter, and Jesus said, basically, I am not sent to dogs, but to the lost sheep of Israel? She immediately agreed that she was a dog. "Yes, Lord, but even the dogs under the table feed on the children's crumbs."[15] She took the Lord's breath away with her swift answer and walked away the mother of a healed child.

When Jesus called people something unpleasant, He was placing a mirror in front of them. "Here, look! You've got dirt all over your face! You need to get cleaned up." Mothers of preschoolers understand this perfectly. I prayed once with a dear friend who saw a picture of a young boy who had a very dirty leg. He was resisting taking a bath. The problem was that the dirt was hiding the severity of the wound beneath it. When Jesus calls attention to dirt, He's pointing with healing hands to the wound beneath. He never uncovers to embarrass, but to heal. His hard words are always an invitation to health.

When Jesus told Peter he was about to deny Him three times, it was not a prediction of fate. It was an invitation for Peter to admit he wasn't ready for what was just around the corner. If Peter had immediately agreed with the diagnosis and asked Jesus to strengthen him, he probably wouldn't have betrayed his Lord.

When Jesus speaks, the intent is always redemption. When we say hard things, it must be redemptive, too.

The language of honor does not ignore reality. It encourages us to get in the bath. The towels are warm, the soap smells sweet and the marriage ceremony is within the hour.

Jesus,

Give us a pure language. Script within us a speech of the heart that is full of honor. Take away our biting humor. Our tongues are often like swords that pierce. Teach us pleasant words. We want the words we say to bring Your life and hope. We want to be truth speakers who are full of Your mercy. We want our words to be a fountain of life. Only You can make it so. Amen.

SCRIPTURES FOR MEDITATION
Proverbs 15:26; 30:5; Psalms 19:14; 119:130

QUESTIONS WORTH ASKING

· Give an example of a recent time when you felt God convict you of your speech. What, if anything, changed in your speech or attitude?
· Find three verses in Proverbs that deal with the power of the tongue. What do these verse say to you?
· Describe someone you know who speaks the language of honor. How do you respond to that person?
· Did Jesus ever diagnose a condition He didn't intend to heal?

Notes
1. Charles R. Swindoll, *The Tale of the Tardy Oxcart* (Nashville: Word Publishing, 1998), p. 518.
2. Acts 23:5 makes it clear that we are not to speak evil of a ruler of our people, even if that ruler is opposing God.
3. Eugene Peterson, *Working the Angles: The Shape of Pastoral Integrity* (Grand Rapids: Eerdmans Publishing Co., 1990), n.p.
4. See James 3:8-10.

5. John 1:1,14, *KJV.*

6. Ken Gire, *Intimate Moments with the Savior* (Grand Rapids, Mich.: Zondervan, 1989), p. 7.

7. Psalm 113:5,6, *NKJV.*

8. Proverbs 15:33, *NKJV.*

9. See Romans 4:17.

10. See Proverbs 11:19.

11. See Matthew 15:26; 23:27; Luke 13:32; John 2:4.

12. G. Campbell Morgan, *Studies in the Prophecy of Jeremiah* (Old Tappan, N.J.: Fleming H. Revell, 1969), p. 10.

13. Matthew 16:16, *NIV.*

14. See Matthew 16:23, *KJV.*

15. Mark 7:28.

CHAPTER FIFTEEN

The Color of Worship

And they sang a new song, saying:
"You are worthy to take the scroll, and to open its seals;
For You were slain,
And have redeemed us to God by Your blood
Out of every tribe and tongue and people and nation."
—Revelation 5:9, NKJV

"You stole my song, and I want it back." The words hung in the air, a pure mercy, considering that the weight of their meaning might have crushed us.

We had gathered from all over the world to simply seek God together for four days. There was no agenda, no Plan B if God didn't show up. We sat in two circles, one within another, in a small retreat room. Wave after wave of repentance thundered over our hearts and our histories. During this session the Holy Spirit seemed to be underscoring the British and their colonization of the world. Richard Twiss, a tall Lakota/Sioux reconciliation leader continued speaking, "You stole my song, and I want it back. I am going to sing it and you are going to give it back to me; you are going to sing it back to me." The three British men he was addressing were too undone to argue.

Richard sang in Lakota a song about traveling the Jesus road. There was a palpable silence. The haunting ancient melody hung over the room like morning fog. Then Stuart McAlpine, a pastor in Washington, D.C., haltingly sang the melody back to Richard. At that point, what little was left of our composure completely unraveled. A Maori brother began to do the Haka, and Stuart again repeated the movements. God swept into the room, the doors to His entrance swinging on the small hinges of simple prophetic acts.

Can you picture commissioning an artist to paint the Body of Christ, and telling him you have one stipulation—that he can only paint with white? The color of worship is astonishing.

Here was our Native American brother, full of dignity and authority, having to ask for the return of his own song—his own personal expression to his Creator—stolen by Western Christians who thought anything native was evil.

I realized afresh how grievous it was that we, as Western Occidentals, had colonized worship and rarely encouraged indigenous worship. We dismissed entire cultures, saying in effect, "If you really want to be godly, be like us, sing like us, preach like us. Be a white man." This was not always intentional, but it was nonetheless sin.

It is true that many of the missionaries who first went to these cultures had hearts that burned with love for the people they served, and we should always honor their memory and sacrifice. But often there has been a hidden presupposition that the Western way is the godly way. We assumed that our way was the superior way because it was familiar. We may have been blissfully unaware of that systemic thing God hates most—our pride.

I have an audiocassette of indigenous worship that I often play in my car. There are many different styles of worship on it, in many different languages. What is amazing is how often it catches the ear of my young son's friends. It's almost as if they're not old enough yet to have had their hearts hardened by ethnocentrism. The deadly crabgrass of cultural arrogance has not yet taken firm hold in the tender soil of their hearts. Their reaction underscores how our pride of culture has impoverished our own ability to worship.

As I have gotten to know and love my indigenous brothers and sisters, I marvel at how many colors God has given us. The color of worship is astonishing. Can you picture commissioning an artist to paint the Body of Christ and telling him you have one stipulation—that he can only paint with white? Can you imagine commissioning a musician to create a symphony with only one stipulation—that he can use only one instrument?

Recently, I attended the World Christian Gathering of Indigenous People, in Rapid City, South Dakota. As I filmed indigenous people from all over the world, I saw firsthand the beauty of God's design in making different cultures. I saw the melodious grace of the Native Hawaiian and the jubilant worship of my Samoan brothers Alfatia and Fia. I saw the poignant worship of the Sammi, indigenous people of Norway, Finland, Russia and Sweden. My heart pounded with resonance as my Maori brothers and sisters did the Haka, their voices fierce with authority. I almost couldn't film for tears as tribe after tribe of Native Americans processed in, each dressed in regalia that King Solomon would have envied. My heart was stunned at what my eyes beheld.

THE BLESSING OF DIFFERENT GIFTS AND TRADITIONS

For too long we have missed the beauty and richness God

intended in creating cultures different from one another. He created the differences to bless us, but we've often used them to ridicule and dominate one another. We have pitted our strengths against other cultures' perceived weaknesses and, in the process, we've robbed ourselves of our own inheritance.

Scripture goes to great lengths to instruct us in the importance of every member of the Body. In 1 Corinthians 12, we have Paul's discussion of the Body of Christ and each member's contribution. Most times, when we think of the term "members," we generally think of a homogenous group. The members of the choir all sing, the members of the Parent-Teacher Organization all have children in a particular school. But when Paul is talking "members," he's purposefully using the word to mean "difference."

Absolute difference. Your brain is nothing like your kidney, and your lungs are nothing like your teeth. The fact that you can read this paragraph is because there are so many different and dissimilar members of your body cooperating together. As you read, your brain is telling your lungs to breathe. Your eyes are transmitting symbols to your mind. Your spirit is wondering if any of my observations are correct. It takes many different parts of you to make it through this paragraph.

We know that no one person can express all of what it means to be made in God's image. It takes many different and distinct personalities to express even a fraction of Him. There are people with thunderous personalities, and people with gentle, meek souls. There are people who are militant, reminding us that our God is a man of war, and people who are peaceable, who remind us that Jesus is the Prince of Peace. There are scholars who never met a fact they didn't like, and practical people who never liked a fact they couldn't apply. Both types show us that God loves to think, and He loves to act. Just as every personality has something to tell us about God, every culture enriches us with their differences and allows us to see the Lord of Hosts more clearly through them.

DRESSING FOR WORSHIP

The apostle John saw how we will worship in heaven. His vision, in the book of Revelation, presents an interesting question. How did he know the people before the throne were from every tribe and tongue? Could it be they actually wore different regalia? Could they have looked different from one another? We don't know. But I suspect that any idea of a homogenous, monocultural Bride may be a huge mistake.

In the books of Daniel and Revelation, it is very clear that there will be people from every nation offering worship before the throne. If God is to be praised by every nation, wouldn't it be reasonable to assume that each nation will present Him with their own distinctive cultural gifts? The Vaglas of Ghana may be playing antelope horns, the Micronesians may be blowing conch shells and the indigenous peoples of Australia may be playing the dijirido. And if that is going to be the state in heaven, shouldn't we be enjoying cultural diversity in our worship experience here?[1] Haven't we prayed that God's will would be done on earth as it is in heaven?

It bears repeating: We cannot display the fascinating character and personality of God with just one culture. As we honor other cultures, finding them to be significant and valuable, we acknowledge our need of each other in order to demonstrate the grace and glory of God. God made our differences to facilitate us seeking and finding Him. He is a God who wants to be found, and He is not far from us.

> He made from one, every nation of mankind to live on all the face of the earth, having determined their appointed times, and the boundaries of their habitation, that they should seek God, if perhaps they might grope for Him and find Him,

though He is not far from each one of us; for in Him we live and move and exist, as even some of your own poets have said, "For we also are His offspring" (Acts 17:26-28).

Paul could have said, "He is not far from us Jews, because we are the chosen people"; but no, he says to a Greek crowd, "He is not far from each of us." Paul honors the Greeks by quoting one of their very own poets.

Paul obviously had to have read Greek poetry in order to quote it. Was he just reading in order to find a point of entrance for the gospel? Could he have actually read it because he might have enjoyed it?

When we honor another culture, we recognize and respond to all that is good in that culture. We don't summarily dismiss it because it is unfamiliar. We recognize that God has specifically placed parts of His personality in every culture for our good and enjoyment.

We are learning to give place to one another, to honor and respect each other's gifts and perspectives. We are beginning to enjoy the beauty and dignity of other cultures. We are coming to learn more about our Father from observing His brilliant character in each other. We are beginning to listen with a careful ear to each other's stories and songs. We are learning to bring joy to God's heart by our enjoyment of one another. We are becoming a demonstration of the manifold (diverse, variegated, multicolored) wisdom of God being shown through the Church to the rulers and authorities in heavenly places.[2]

PRAYING OTHER CULTURES INTO THEIR INHERITANCE

All over the world, God is underscoring His desire to be worshiped by all tribes and tongues. As we come to understand God's passion for all cultures, we will yearn to see them become all that God has ever wanted them to become. We will want to see God's holy ambition fulfilled. We will want other cultures to experience the full gamut of the grace and glory of Jesus Christ. One of the best ways to honor anyone is to pray them into their inheritance.

One Korean pastor, Reverend Sung Hong, has prayed for 25 years and now has recruited 1 million Korean women to pray for the world's indigenous peoples. In the past few years, a God-breathed prayer movement has spread like wildfire. Children in well-developed networks throughout the world[3] are praying for the people in the 10/40 Window.[4] When we pray for other cultures, we are saying that we want what God wants—people from every tribe and tongue to worship Him. When we pray this way, we are acknowledging our incompleteness without our brothers and sisters of other cultures.

The whole point of history and the various cultures is the romancing of God to woo and win a bride for His Son, and He has always intended for His Bride to be multicultural. That became evident on the day of Pentecost, the birthday of the Church.

The Bible is clear and consistent on this subject: There will be more people than anyone can count from every tribe, tongue and nation, worshiping before the throne. There won't be a Samoan Night on Tuesdays and a Swedish Night on Wednesdays, and then you have the Italians singing opera on Thursdays. We will sing together a new song; we will stand together shoulder-to-shoulder. Together we will enjoy the pleasures of God forever.

New Zealander David Garret, a father of the praise and worship movement, observes:

Not only is the Father looking through the Earth for worshipers (see John 4:23,24), but worship itself will become one of the greatest "tools" in bringing the

nations of the earth to him....The nations have had
worship stolen from them by the prince of the power of
the air, who was even prepared to give the nations away
to be worshiped by Jesus. God is calling for the worship
of the nations to be returned to Him.

Linked with that, peoples are not going to be
content with secondhand music. More and more indigenous peoples are going to want to express something to
God that really expresses their deepest hearts. As
"worship in spirit and truth" is given back to the Creator
from every tribe, and in every language, I believe this will
be one of the greatest evangelistic tools ever seen.[5]

WHEN WE HONOR ALL

As we learn to *honor each other*, we will know a depth of God
unavailable to us any other way.

In *honoring God*, we will come to know the reason for which
we are made.

In *honoring God's Word*, we will come to know the contours of
God's fascinating heart and mind.

In *honoring the relationships* God has given us, we will come to
understand God's unswerving commitment to us.

God has indeed fixed His eye upon us and made us the
objects of His attentive affection. Through honor we model that
love to each other. By honor we are prepared for eternity. By
honor we understand the future that awaits us.

As we seriously pursue honoring other cultures, we will see the
beauty and grace and dignity that God has given each for the enjoyment of all. And we will join the great multicolored throng before
the throne, saying, Glory and honor and strength to the Lamb!

Worthy Lamb,

We are honored to love You. And our hearts burn within us to offer You a song worthy of Your great and awesome glory. We need each other, because none of us can sing the song and do it justice by ourselves. A trumpet does not make a symphony, and one culture can never adequately sound Your praise. One color does not a painting make. And so You have gifted us with each other out of every tribe and tongue. And so we will build a ring around Your throne, O Lamb. We will sing for worlds without end of Your excellence. We will joy in Your glory, honor and strength forever. Amen.

SCRIPTURES FOR MEDITATION

Psalm 8:5; Acts 17:26-28; 1 Corinthians 12; Ephesians 3:10; 1 Peter 2:17

Notes
1. For an excellent treatment on this subject, read Richard Twiss's book *Five Hundred Years of Bad Haircuts,* available from Wiconi International, P.O. Box 5246, Vancouver, Wash. 98668 (360) 546-1867.
2. See Ephesians 3:10.
3. Cheri Fuller, *When Children Pray* (Sisters, Oreg.: Multnomah Publishers, 1998), p. 161.
4. The 10/40 Window is comprised of the 62-plus countries between the northern latitudes of 10 and 40 degrees, often called the least evangelized countries in the world.
5. *Global Worship Report, I* (January 1999), no. 8, from the AD2000 Worship and Arts Network. Prior editions of the *Global Worship Report* can be found on the AD2000 website at http://www.ad2000.org/tracks/worship. To contact David Garret, e-mail: 75231.2321@compuserve.com.

Praying by Listening

Many people all over the world have found that the following steps open up to them a whole new dimension in prayer. I remember first hearing them on the island of Guam, almost 25 years ago. My prayer life was drastically altered, and I have never been the same.

ACKNOWLEDGE WHO YOU ARE ADDRESSING

You have been invited into the presence of the magnificent Son of God, Jesus, the glory of the Church, who dominates the entire universe.

INVITE PERSONAL CLEANSING

Invite the Holy Spirit to search your heart and reveal specific areas of sin, such as apathy, unbelief, spiritual pride or presumption. Accept readily God's cleansing and forgiveness.

DEAL FIRMLY
WITH THE ENEMY

Take authority over all powers that would seek to distract
and inhibit your prayer. Arm yourself with the all-powerful
name of Jesus and the Word of God.

PACK UP YOUR
PERSONAL CONCERNS

Hand over all your own personal prayer burdens, no matter
how pressing, trusting God to undertake for you as you
pray as the Holy Spirit directs.

MEDITATE
ON THE WORD

The Bible is the perfect prayer book. As we take time to let
God's words seep into our spirit, we find God giving us
prayers from His heart.

PRAY WHAT
GOD GIVES YOU

Be bold to speak out whatever God gives you from your
meditation on the Word. God may give you a simple picture
or Scripture or the name of a country or person.
Continue to ask for direction.

Covenant of Unity

One significant way we can honor each other is through covenant. In recognition that Jesus has only one Church that meets in many congregations, many pastors have adopted this particular covenant. In Psalm 133, we see the link between unity and anointing. Cities that are experiencing the blessing of God are cities where spiritual leaders are committed to honor each other.

SOMEBODY CARES® ANY TOWN

We believe Jesus Christ has one Church, His beloved Bride, for whom He gave Himself. The Church of Jesus Christ in (your city) is comprised of many believers and congregations throughout the city. Jesus has sanctified and cleansed her with the washing of the Word of God so that she might be presented to Him, a glorious Church without spot or wrinkle.

Christ has committed the care, cleansing and preparation of the Bride to us as shepherds. Endeavoring to keep unity of the Spirit in the bond of peace, we solemnly and joyfully enter into this covenant, pledging that by God's grace we shall:

- Love God with our all, and the Church fervently, doing all things in love.
- Pray for and encourage each other and our congregations on a regular basis.
- Speak well of one another at all times, especially in our preaching and teaching, putting to silence those who would be used by the adversary to spread evil reports among us.
- Hold one another accountable in regard to lifestyle, integrity and devotional life, meeting together regularly.
- Keep the bond of peace within the Body of Christ by carefully receiving members who have informed their previous church leaders as to their leaving, seeking to resolve any conflict to the best of their ability.
- Be real and transparent with one another, resisting the temptation to impress each other with our size, abilities or accomplishments.
- Advertise in a manner that is positive for the whole Bride of Christ, and not self-promoting at the expense of other churches or ministries.
- Respect and pursue relationships with those who may be of different distinctives. We are crossing racial and denominational lines, meeting at the Cross. We believe in the essentials, unity; in the nonessentials, liberty; and in all things, love.
- Follow the Good Shepherd's example by giving our lives for God's flock in (your city).
- Prepare the Bride for the return of the Bridegroom, Jesus Christ, by mobilizing our members and promoting area-wide strategies and programs designed to evangelize and impact our city with the gospel of Jesus Christ.

While men reach for thrones to build their own
kingdoms, Jesus reached for a towel to wash men's feet.

—Doug Stringer, Founder

Somebody Cares® America

Somebody Cares® America is a ministry of Turning Point Ministries International, P.O. Box 570663, Houston, TX 77257-0663. Phone: 713-621-1498; fax: 713-621-2076; e-mail: tpmail@tpmi.org. Used by permission.

Our Hands Are Stained

Someone once said that the history of the Jews is God's love letter to the world. Yet instead of honoring the Jews, the Church has often been a malicious part of their history. Around the world, Christians are responding to the Holy Spirit's conviction about our grievous past and our need to humble ourselves and repent.

This Service of Repentance is an excellent scriptural confession of our need to honor and affirm God's chosen people.

Although Your Word says of Your chosen people, the Jews, they are beloved for the sake of their forefathers (Rom. 11:28), love has not been characteristic of Christianity's attitude toward the Jewish people these past two thousand years.

O Lord our God, we confess our lack of love. Forgive us, we pray.

From earliest times we have adopted toward the Jews a loveless, arrogant and critical attitude, foreign to the spirit of Jesus. We have not remembered Your Word:

> Do not boast over those branches....You do not support the root, but the root supports you. Do not be arrogant, but be afraid (Rom. 11:18,20, *NIV*).

O Lord our God, we confess our spiritual arrogance. Forgive us, we pray.

And the New Testament states unequivocally:

God has not rejected his people whom he foreknew (Rom. 11:2).

O Lord our God, we confess our spiritual blindness. Forgive us, we pray.

Instead of sympathizing, instead of weeping with those who weep, we have actually increased the sufferings of the Jews—and this in spite of Your warning:

I have begun to punish my own people, so should you go free? No, you shall not evade punishment. (Jer. 25:29, *TLB*)

O Lord our God, we confess that we have increased the sufferings of Your chosen people. Forgive us, we pray.

May our hearts ache to see this chosen people of God, wandering through the centuries wretched, despised, shunned, ostracized and afflicted with pain like the suffering of God in Isaiah 53. Then, looking on them we will be reminded of You, our Lord and Savior.

Forgive us for not seeing in Your people a reflection of You, Lord Jesus.

Though You are called the consolation of Israel, we have made Your name repulsive to the Jewish people because of the many atrocities committed in Your name.

Forgive us for discrediting You and bringing shame upon Your name, Lord Jesus.

Unlike the Good Samaritan, we so often looked the other way when Your people were in need. But what we do to the least of Your brothers we do to You. And so it was You we have failed and grieved.

Forgive us for failing to fulfill the divine mandate to show love and mercy, Lord Jesus.

The prophet Zechariah says:

He who touched you [Israel] touches the apple of his [God's] eye (Zech. 2:8).

And the prophet Isaiah writes:

In all their affliction he was afflicted (Isa. 63:9).

Although we cannot undo centuries of evil, may we be truly repentant and, in that spirit of true repentance, find ways of expressing love. Give us, we pray, the right attitude to our Jewish brothers and sisters.

We pause to reflect on the past centuries. In deep shame we silently remember:

The Crusades of the Middle Ages, when Jews were burnt alive in Jerusalem's synagogue by Crusaders singing, "Christ we adore Thee," in the belief they were avenging the death of Christ.

The practice of segregating Jews into ghettos and forcing them to wear the badge of shame—a forerunner of the Yellow Star.

The forcing of Jews to undergo baptism as an alternative to exile or death.

The false accusations of ritual murder, costing thousands of innocent lives, sometimes wiping out an entire Jewish population.

The Inquisition, which consigned Jews to death by burning at the stake. An estimated 30,000 Marranos perished in the flames.

The pogroms, occurring on Christian holidays such as Christmas and Easter, when Jewish men and women were beaten to death with crosses.

The prejudices shaped by theology, causing many.of us, or our parents and grandparents, either to give tacit consent to the persecution of the Jews during the Holocaust or to remain indifferent to their plight. Very few Christians helped our Jewish brothers and sisters in the hour of their greatest need.

Lord, have mercy.

Christ, have mercy. Lord, have mercy and forgive us our guilt toward Your chosen people.

Used by permission of Evangelical Sisterhood of Mary, Darnstadt, Germany. For more information contact: Evangelical Sisterhood of Mary, 9849 N. 40th St., Phoenix, Arizona, 85028.